In the schools of the world, youth introduced to science become atheists. Through the mass media we are taught that science has proved we no longer need God to understand the universe. In the movement called "Higher Criticism" theologians try to adjust religion to science and arrive at a conclusion contrary to our faith. In all walks of life the victory of science over religion is loudly proclaimed.

Must science and religion contradict each other?

Does science have any evidence or proof that religion and God belong to the realm of myths and legends? Is the supernatural only the product of our imagination? Or is it real, with science only astutely used to prevent our reaching real knowledge?

This book is a concise critical examination of science: from an historical perspective. This book is not another book of apologetics that seeks to reconcile the Bible with the latest findings or theories of science. For the Bible is not obliged to catch up with science; on the contrary, science must mature within the wisdom of the Bible. This book presents a new world view or philosophy of science revealing that our knowledge from a distance doesn't seem as great as those who use it cleverly against God would like us to believe. This book is full of useful new ideas on how science and religion can be reconciled.

Atheism, or scientism, is the ultimate lie of Satan, the fabled apple of knowledge that brought about our downfall in the first place. Still, it is not science itself that is evil, but rather the false, atheistic interpretation of it. Put in a proper perspective, science can strengthen our faith.

The tide is turning in our days. Atheism reached its twilight and atheistic science its dead end. The future belongs to those who can reconcile God with science, thus freeing science from the bondage of atheism that in our days has prevented its further development. Not only does science not contradict religion, but religion can in fact shed new light on our knowledge, since the source of all knowledge is God.

Stephen A. Foglein

THE APPLE OF KNOWLEDGE

An inquiry about God and science

By
Stephen A. Foglein

ATLAS BOOKS PUBLISHING COMPANY
P.O. Box 844
Mountain View, California 94042
1981

Copyright © 1981 by Stephen A. Foglein.
All rights reserved.

Printed and bound in the United States of America.

ATLAS BOOKS PUBLISHING COMPANY
P.O. Box 844
Mountain View, CA 94042

Editor: Helen Tartar
Design and Typesetting: Jane Arnovick,
 Editorial Associates, Los Altos
Printing: Book Crafters, Inc.

CONTENTS

    Introduction 1

1. The War that Gave Birth to Modern Science 11
2. Basic Sciences: Physics, Chemistry, Biology 21
3. Our Knowledge About the Universe: Astronomy .40
4. New Perspectives in Astronomy:
   The Death of Materialism 50
5. Evolution: A Truth or a Lie?
   Introduction to Dimension 59
6. Geology: The Knowledge of Our Planet Earth . .71
7. Man Appears on Earth. 84
8. Is History an Exact Science? 96
9. The Dubious Blessings of Progress. 108
10. Psychology and Its Effect on Our Life 118
11. What's Wrong with Science? 130
12. Where is God in This Vastly Expanded
    Universe?. 144

    Conclusion 157

    Bibliography 162

INTRODUCTION

Science has become the greatest force shaping our lives. Every segment of life is affected by it. Without proper education, including at least an introduction to science, it is becoming increasingly difficult for an individual to find an appropriate place in society. For the first time in the history of mankind, in the United States education through maturity at the age of eighteen is offered freely to everyone, regardless of sex, race, or any other background consideration. Many great men of previous ages dreamed about such a wide educational opportunity. They thought knowledge would lift up mankind, that it would eliminate ignorance, poverty, and misery. But in practice this has not been the case.

Science and education have failed somewhere. Our schools are producing youths who no longer value traditional moral laws. Increasingly cynical, they expect too much without supposing themselves obliged to make a significant contribution. On the most basic values of mankind, summed up by religion, they have a negative atheistic view that they have picked up in the schools, where mention of God's name and His laws is forbidden, while atheistic dogmas are freely taught in the name of secularism.

Atheists claim that science has provided them with proofs that religion and the idea of God are only superstitions, based on the ignorance of previous ages. Since our knowledge has increased, they say, we no longer need those ideas. God, redemption, and original sin, together with Jesus, all belong to the realm of myths and fairy tales.

Do they know something we don't? Are we Christians simply ignorant about such matters, and is this the reason we still cling to our outdated convictions? Does science really have undeniable evidence that our view is obsolete? Or does science not have any real proof at all to support its claims, so that all atheist ideas are based on false interpretations of our limited knowledge?

In our days some theologians, even, tend to accept the new scientific outlook on life. They would like to reconcile religion with this new truth, and in the process, called the "Higher

INTRODUCTION

Criticism," they hopelessly lose their faith. Science and theology have been at war during the past few centuries, and theology lost the battle. But does this mean that we have lost the war, too? In our days atheists proclaim the victory of science over theology, but the war is not yet over! Seemingly, the tide is turning. People no longer believe in atheistic dogmas, and evidence that the atheist view is no longer valid is piling up. Darwinism, falsely called evolution, is questioned by many. Parents are organizing to protest the one-sided teaching of atheistic dogmas in schools maintained by their tax dollars.

The key to the present-day controversy lies in science itself. An examination of our scientific knowledge reveals that science has no proof at all to contradict religion and the idea of God. Quite the contrary. But science is used assiduously against these ideas, the most basic inheritance of humankind.

In this book I intend to reexamine science in a light that cannot be found anywhere else. This inquiry will shed new light on science, from a point of view opposite that found in present-day scientific books, most of which are written by atheists to further their aims. In this book I intend to point out the weaknesses of our knowledge, which others carefully hide. However, we should not be afraid of the truth. Anyone courageous enough to follow me in this journey will see that our knowledge is very limited, highly uncertain, and plagued with false ideas and misconceptions that have been blown out of proportion.

Any such review of scientific knowledge is bound to produce new ideas by discovering hidden, perhaps carefully shielded, connections within science. Of course in such a small book I can give only a bird's-eye view, but I hope that the new ideas in this book may prove worthy of further development, and that they can serve as the foundation of a necessary reexamination of natural philosophy. I have not been able to go into detail, although sometimes the temptation was almost irresistible. Instead, I have sought simplicity, to avoid the scientific jargon that makes the reading of scientific books a boring, wearisome task, since only a few scientists understand the meaning of the terms they use. I believe this book can be understood by anyone, even by those who lack formal scienti-

INTRODUCTION

tific training. The ideas in the book are free for scientists to use, too. I would myself welcome the opportunity to work out some of my ideas, but I confess to having little hope of working them out in detail.

Who can benefit from reading this book? I believe anyone can who has any doubt about the truths of religion that are based on scientific claims. It should be especially useful for youth, who are saturated one-sidedly with the false, atheistic explanations of science. It could also be useful for students of theology, priests, teachers—anyone who has an open mind and an affinity for the truth, and who has not yet been hopelessly brainwashed.

This book is a concise examination of our knowledge, which from a distance doesn't appear as great as the atheists want us to believe. I hope it will trigger more intense research within science, for all branches of science cry out for detailed reexamination. Today atheistic ideas block the further development of scientific knowledge. Any scientist who has an open mind and will undertake such a reexamination will profit from it greatly and will be able to write his name permanently in the history of science. I urge all decent scientists to undertake the great task of freeing science from the bondage of atheism. The reward will be greater than can be imagined.

I would not dare to undertake such a huge task as reexamining our knowledge if I was not convinced by research in my own field that such a venture is possible. It isn't mere coincidence that today's most broadly atheistic outlook on science is represented by Carl Sagan. Like me, he is a geologist and an astronomer. These two branches of science, in contrast to the narrow specializations common today, require a background of broad knowledge of the findings of many other areas of science, thus giving an individual the training to see things in perspective. By reexamining my own field I have found many new, still-hidden connections that shed new light on all scientific knowledge. This prompted me to write this book, a skeleton of a new worldview that can change our whole outlook on the universe.

I have arrived at exactly the opposite conclusion to that of Sagan. While he and others try to convince us that an under-

INTRODUCTION

standing of the universe does not require the existence of God, I am convinced that exactly the opposite is true. If we strip science of false and deliberately misleading atheistic explanations—as this book intends to do—we not only have a greater need for a Creator, but without Him we can understand nothing!

Let us now start on this journey into the vast realm of science in search of the essence of our knowledge, without prejudice. We need not be afraid of the truth. The truth is God and He can be found everywhere. Our objective is to uncover the truth, and to ask the question whether or not it supports the fashionable atheistic ideas proclaimed in the name of science in our days.

1

THE WAR THAT GAVE BIRTH TO MODERN SCIENCE

A few basic questions have occupied the minds of men since ancient times. Some of these questions, to mention only a few, are: Who are we in relation to our surroundings? Was man always on earth, or does mankind have a beginning and, consequently, an end? Why is there suffering in life and, eventually, death, and what happens to us after we die? What is the nature that surrounds us? What are the bright, mysterious stars? Such questions are considered to be philosophical, and the answers people have arrived at are very complicated. Like many other problems in life, these questions have many plausible answers, and in different ages people have offered different ones. Each individual, at one time or another, is bound to give some kind of answer to each of these questions, and the answer he accepts will influence his whole life.

Throughout history, from the earliest times, men have held a firm belief that we are not alone in the universe. There are beings above us, and these beings have an effect on our life. Even peoples of the most primitive cultures, like the aborigines of Australia, know the existence of these higher beings, and in their ceremonies try to please them. From the earliest times these supernatural beings have been divided into two categories: forces of good and of evil. Throughout the ages men have known that life doesn't end with death, that it will continue on a higher level. Men knew that life on earth couldn't be the result of a casual accident, but that it was created by a being who is above all that is seen and unseen, and He sees to it that the universe goes on in an orderly fashion, according to His Will.

These basic values are the cornerstones of all religions, from the most primitive to the highest, Christianity. Religions in different parts of the world have built elaborate systems starting from these basic truths. And although these systems may vary in their ideas of how to please the supernatural forces or how to prepare the individual for a better afterlife, there is considerable consistency in their basic values.

Almost all religions know that men existed on a higher plane before their present status, and that their fall from this higher plane is a direct consequence of disobeying the Creator. All religions, no matter how distant from each other, know as an historical fact that at one time mankind was almost completely annihilated by a flood or Deluge raging on a worldwide scale, and that only one family escaped that major catastrophe.

Men, though very similar to the other members of the animal kingdom, still differ considerably from them. Men have the ability to create things. Men do not possess natural weapons to defend themselves. Their offspring require much more time to reach maturity than those of the animals, and the offspring need elaborate care. Such disadvantages can be overcome only by group living and cooperation. Every group has to have a leader, a coordinating will, which eventually leads to specialization of tasks. As the number of men increased on earth, the family groups grew into larger tribes and later into nations and empires, which coordinated the tribes of a large territory. This brought forth the possibility of further specialization. Some men, freed from the daily chores of life, were able to devote all their time to the basic questions of life. From primitive signs, writing was developed to record the essential beliefs of men, and later to record significant events and the deeds of a great ruler; thus history began.

One of the earliest known cultures was Mesopotamia, between the Tigris and Euphrates rivers. From that area a peculiar race sprang forth, who trace back their origin to one man called Abraham. They left an extensive record of their history and beliefs, which became the foundation of our civilization, what we call the Bible. The writing of the Bible was initiated by one of the greatest leaders of this race, a man called Moses. Moses, according to the written documents, was a highly educated man.

He was well versed in the accumulated knowledge of the Egyptian culture. Later, when he became the leader of his own race, the Jews, he certainly became familiar with the Jewish traditions and knowledge originating in Mesopotamia. Moses led his people out from slavery in Egypt. He formed them into a conquering force in order to occupy the promised land, which we know as Israel. In his books, besides the record of their miraculous escape from the well-organized Egyptian empire, and the laws necessary to govern the life of the newly formed nation, he gives a brief account of all knowledge accumulated before his time, an account of the creation of the universe, of man, and a brief history of mankind. This first part of the Bible is called Genesis.

One of the most essential parts of Genesis is the story of the Fall of Man, and in connection with this, God's promise to restore the former status of men through a Messiah. Christianity is founded on that promise.

Throughout the centuries, God governed His chosen people through prophets. The prophecies are the most important parts of the Bible. The prophets always kept alive the hope of a coming redeemer, but the centuries passed by and the Messiah just did not come. The Jews became prey to newly emerging powers like the Babylonians and later the Romans, and they lost their statehood. When they were in this wretched condition, conquered and overrun by the Romans, there came a man called Jesus who, despite his lowly origin and his trade as a carpenter, claimed for himself the title of Messiah.

The Jews rejected this claim, declaring him dangerous to the nation, and handed him to the occupying Roman forces to be put to death. But all efforts to suppress the teachings of this dangerous "blasphemer" were in vain. The death of Jesus gave rise to a very powerful movement, soon to conquer the whole known world, even the Roman Empire and, in turn, its vandal conquerors, to flourish undisturbed for more than a thousand years. Thus Christianity was born.

Christianity is based on Judaism. Jesus didn't want to give us a brand new religion. His most important message was that through Him God is reconciled with mankind. He said He was going to heaven to prepare for us a new home, where after death we will be with Him and, in a new, eternal life, will enjoy eternal happiness, a happiness not even imaginable on earth. He also warned us that life on earth is a test, full of temptations. God's enemy Satan will do anything to keep us from reaching heaven. Therefore, whoever wants to follow Him must restrain himself in this life and concentrate all efforts on finding the way to heaven. Those who fail the test and join the enemy will go to hell, a place of eternal suffering.

No wonder that during the Middle Ages Christians were occupied with the afterlife, and completely neglected the life on earth! Who cares about the shadow of reality if he can keep his eyes on reality itself; who cares about a life full of tears and sorrow when the real one starts after a brief journey in this valley of tears?

Such thoughts occupied the minds of the majority, but in all societies there are men who try to approach questions from a different angle. Such men tried to reconcile the simple teachings of Christianity with ancient pagan theories of philosophy, astronomy, and science to gain a full knowledge of God; thus theology was born, which in plain English means "knowledge of God." In this way scientific speculations—bound to change in time—were welded together with the basic and clear truth of Christ's teaching.

One may love God, but no one ever will be able to know Him. St. Augustine knew that; he knew that, just as the sea cannot be bailed into a small pit, so the knowledge of the Creator of the infinite universe cannot be comprehended by our small, limited minds. But efforts were made to do just that. The picture that was created can be compared to the drawing of a small child who ventures to draw a man.

The most pleasing picture of the universe is the one created by St. Thomas Aquinas. It is based on the pagan astronomy of Ptolemy, who thought that the center of the universe was the earth. Though the vulnerable Ptolemaic basis of Aquinas's system has been breached, the essence of his theory still holds, because it is perfect. Since his time the material universe as we know it has extended its boundaries, but we still are not able to refute the existence of God above the material universe. St. Thomas Aquinas pictured the universe with God above all. Immediately under Him are the angels, three kinds of them. The first group attends God's throne; the second, the physical universe; and the third, the earth and its inhabitants. Then comes the earth and men. Below the earth is hell, where the rebellious angels reside with their chief, Lucifer, who formerly was one of the highest-ranking angels. These evil spirits can still move freely around the universe to create trouble for the good angels, and to stir up trouble between nations and people; they are responsible for the temptations to sin, and they cause disorders in nature, such as hailstorms and drought, as part of the punishment of mankind.

In the Middle Ages, any kind of science that went beyond this was considered useless. As Cardinal Baronius put it: "The intention of the Holy Ghost is to teach us how one goes to heaven, not how heaven goes." Medicine was considered to be cheating the will of God, who sent the suffering to be punished or to gain merit. Astronomy survived as part of astrology, which still flourished as an amusement for the King and to predict and explain the signs of Heaven, such as comets, and to record the changes of the year. In the making of a proper calendar, it was entirely indifferent whether the earth went around the sun, or the sun went around the earth. The latter was self-evident—anybody could see that not the earth but the sun moved. All phenomena had a supernatural explanation, as they had from the beginning.

This was a perfect world understandable by everybody and accepted by everybody. The Pope as the head of Church was the spiritual head of all Christians, including the kings and emperors, who also were Christians and therefore were under the spiritual jurisdiction of the Pope. Of course life was not that smooth, for troubles always exist, but the general idea was perfect.

Then came the Renaissance, the rebirth of pagan culture, philosophy, literature, and art, and the thousand years' peaceful development of Christianity was over. More and more, men took their eyes from heaven and focused on earth. The Renaissance changed considerably the way of thinking. Men who earlier had readily sacrificed their lives to gain in exchange the Eternal One suddenly discovered the sweet pleasures of earthly life. Instead of sacrificing the body, they started to give to it whatever it desired, and whatever they could afford. At first, of course, these new ideas affected only the most affluent members of society, the kings and the aristocrats, but unfortunately, since the princes of the Church came from among them, the higher ranks of the Church hierarchy were no exception.

Fancy, expensive clothing became the fashion, gorgeous palaces were built, and artists were employed to decorate them and to entertain their inhabitants. Cities became swollen with the new breed of people whose task was to manufacture goods to cater to the fancies of the aristocrats. Thus a new class was born.

Adapting the pagan, mainly Greek and Roman, ways of life and thinking, these aristocrats, princes, and kings gradually became skeptical about religious truths. Soon they started to question the authority of the Church over them. In the Middle Ages the Pope was the highest authority in the Christian world, like the Supreme Court in the United States. This international authority of the universal (catholic) Church soon was challenged by emerging nationalism. Machiavelli can be seen as the father of the separation of church and state. He was the one who stated first that the state has priority over the church in all matters. Rulers soon became greedy for Church property, and started to confiscate it, and to block the collection of Church taxes. The new goods required more money, and they grasped for it wherever they could lay their hands on it. At the same time, they increased the burden of the peasants. All over the Christian world the spirit of rebellion filled the air, and from time to time it produced small-scale revolutions all over Europe. In questioning the authority of the Church, many aristocrats started to question the authority of the rulers of the world, too. A general chaos and disintegration was taking place all over the Christian world.

As we have seen, the first target of the worldly rulers was the earthly property of the Church, but soon her spiritual authority became the subject of profane inquiry, which leads us to the open rebellion of Luther against the spiritual authority of the Church. Behind the Iron Curtain, the Reformation is taught as the first real revolution cloaked in a religious mantle. Judging it in historical perspective, this appears to be true. The princes and the newly emerged middle class were not interested in the sacraments of the Church, but they were very interested in its silverware. For them the Reformation seemed to be the best opportunity to free themselves from the hated yoke of the Church, and at the same time to acquire a perfect ideological cover for their actions.

Both the temporal power and the spiritual power of the Church were destroyed. No wonder that in such an atmosphere the knowledge of God (theology) also became the subject of heated debates. The most vulnerable part of theology was the pagan theories it had adopted, first of all the theory of Ptolemy, the earth-centered, or geocentric, cosmology. Copernicus, with his heliocentric theory, caused an earthquake that shattered the foundation of the accepted theology of St. Thomas Aquinas. And that shattering coincided with the Reformation. These two major blows set the Church, together with all accepted values, on a course that eventually led her to defeat and humiliation, in our own century.

With Copernicus, science started a war against religious truth. Science went on triumphantly to achieve a complete victory and, in our days, the unconditional surrender of theology. In our days Christianity is regarded in scientific circles as a major obstacle to scientific progress, which blocked the way for the development of science for a thousand years, as Gibbon, a philosopher, put it in the last century. A.D. White in *A History of Warfare of Science with Theology in Christendom* went a little further at the end of the last century, calling the saints of the Church mild mental cases who saw hallucinations; the father of psychology, Freud, generalized this idea by calling religion a mass neurosis to be cured; and Marx called it simply the opiate of the masses.

The tendency of the scientific war—or revolution, if you like—is clear: destroy religious truth and replace it with new perspectives, views, theories, and hypotheses entirely different from beliefs men have held so far, replace it with an outlook on a universe where God no longer has any place.

The first target of this war was the Old Testament, particularly Genesis. Science tried to give a secular explanation of the origin of earth and the universe to disprove the old belief in the creation of them by God. If the universe was not created by God, it is quite natural that man wasn't created by Him either. Thus the fall of man and the theory of original sin were declared legend, also, and thus redemption from original sin is a misconception. The great success of science in disproving the Old Testament, using particularly the work of Darwin, led finally to disproving the New Testament, in the form of the "Higher Criticism." A theory that today is widely accepted by many theologians, Protestant and Catholic alike, degrades Jesus Christ to the status of simply a good man, just another founder of a successful religion, who—if He lived at all—was anything but the Son of God. He was the victim of a misconception, deeply embedded in the minds of people at that time, namely, that men had to be redeemed from original sin, and to accomplish this He voluntarily sacrificed his life, of course in vain. The miracles that were attributed to him are only legends invented later by his followers, like the prophecies of the Old Testament, according to a law governing the growth of myths and legends.

The war was long and bitter. The Church first tried in vain to suppress the new thoughts. The Church was always on the defensive, and this proved to be fatal. It was not possible to defend the vulnerable pagan ideas unfortunately incorporated into theology. Defeat on that ground was inevitable, and this defeat left the Church defenseless on other grounds, which opened up the way to the destruction of essential truths that ought to have been defended at any cost.

A question arises: Is science the enemy of religion?

The answer must be an emphatic no! Science is not the enemy of religion, rather science was and is *used* by the enemy of God very shrewdly, even by falsification if need be, to seduce mankind, to turn us against God, the source of all real knowledge and consequently of science. Science can be used to prove the truth of God exactly twice as well as to disprove it, as the great scientist and saint Pascal showed in his works, using the methods of probability. The probability that God exists is two to one. If science can be used to prove religious truth, we ought to try to use it that way. We have to come off of the defensive, and use the tools science has provided for us to prove that our enemies were wrong, and we were right. This book is the first step in that direction.

First we have to admit our defeat, count our resources, and examine critically the achievement of science as it is today. We don't have to attack science; instead we have to show science how it can achieve higher levels if it is able to rid itself of materialism coupled with atheism, which like a straitjacket prevents its further development today. Many basic laws of science were formulated in the heated atmosphere of the war against theology, and often they were based on infinite hatred of God and religion. Many of them no longer represent valid conceptions, forming barricades against further development and progress. Today, these laws must be reexamined before science can develop further.

Many are afraid to criticize science because of the widely held misconception that our knowledge is so vast that not even one discipline of science can be examined or overviewed by a single person. This is a myth designed to protect those who misuse science and do not want to be exposed. Nor should we respect scientific authorities when they defend wrong conceptions. Authority in science unfortunately achieved higher regard than the dogmas of the Church in earlier times. In science, authority cannot block progress, unless it denies completely its essence, open-minded, free thinking. Science cannot sanction sacrosanct ideas; a new idea must supersede the old one if it offers a better-suiting explanation of the universe.

There is another myth: that man is able to know all the secrets of the universe. This idea involves a paradox. Our knowledge can increase, can improve with time and effort, but as we are finite in time, at least in this form, our mind is finite also, and so is our knowledge compared with the infinite universe. Massive barriers confront the expansion of our knowledge.

The atheists accuse Christianity of blocking the free development of scientific thought for a thousand years. It is only polite to say that this statement is grossly unfounded. If the slightest truth is in this statement, then science would be most developed outside of the Christian world, for example in the Arabic world or in India, China, or Japan, and Christianity would be the last stronghold of "darkness," to be conquered by the shining light of science. But the development of science outside Christianity was modest indeed. Why? Because science was born as the daughter of theology, nourished and cared for in its infancy by Christianity. Should we forget that the first temples of learning and research, the first universities, were established by the Church in those very "dark" Middle Ages? Without this tender care, science would have died. The separation of science from its mother is artificial. It is the result of the clever manipulations of the enemies of God. Science and knowledge in general will always be only a part of the greater knowledge of God or, in other words, theology. Everything is the handiwork of the Creator, even if we no longer take this statement literally. When we recognize a law in the universe, we do not invent it. It was there before men set foot on earth, because God wisely placed it there. We have filched all we know from God. We should be humble students of nature, the created work, but we are shortsighted or blind because we no longer want to recognize the teacher, the Creator; we want to believe that we never had a teacher or Creator at all.

In the next chapters I intend to examine the main features of science to see what basis science offers for our infinite pride, which leads us to deny the Creator. Of course I can't go into details, but it really is not necessary to do so. Most books dealing with knowledge start from the broad theories of the universe. After much thought, I decided to start from a more solid ground, the knowledge we gather from our surroundings. This seems logical, since the speculations about the larger universe are only enormous enlargements, unfounded magnifications, of this knowledge, based on the false assumption that what we learned here is applicable to the whole universe—one of the false basic laws of science.

2

BASIC SCIENCES: PHYSICS, CHEMISTRY, BIOLOGY

Almost all basic sciences are in some way the offspring of physics, chemistry, and biology. Though their origins differ, in our days these three sciences are merging into one, since our surroundings basically have been built up from atoms, discovered and dealt with by physics.

The initial progress of these sciences was made possible by the application of measurements in experiments. By measuring different aspects of a phenomenon, a scientist was able to translate it into quantitative terms—that is, to reduce it to numerical expressions, then use mathematical operations to uncover hidden relationships in its behavior. These relationships proved to be laws governing the behavior of the objects examined. As the measuring devices improved and became more complex, it became more and more clear that our world obeys a complex set of laws.

In previous ages, basic physical phenomena were attributed to personified supernatural forces, like angels. The discovery of these new laws shocked mankind. The old explanations, dating back to when men first thought about the world and made an attempt to understand it, became hopelessly naive and outdated, if not downright ridiculous. Many were convinced that religion was wrong, not only in these few proven cases, but as a whole system of values. They believed that in time, science would be able to prove that all conceptions of religion were wrong, and that science would provide a simple, adequate explanation of the whole universe. Thus a brand-new outlook on life—materialism—was born, an outlook that at first only doubted, but later denied, all the values of religious thinking, together with its central premise, God. Thus modern atheism was born, and it became the basic philosophy of science. The goal of science was to prove that religion is wrong, that the Bible is a collection of myths and legends, and that nothing in it is true. These "enlightened" materialists waged war against all religious beliefs, using every conceivable method to drive out the "misconceptions" of religion and God from the society. Every new discovery of science immediately was shaped into a weapon in the hands of these diligent crusaders of "progress and light," a weapon to be used against the dark, reactionary forces of religion. Many of the misconceptions of these zealots still burden science, in the form of distorted basic laws, overemphasizing one side of the phenomenon that proves them right, but neglecting equally important ones that might cast doubt on the validity of their explanation. In physics we still are not able to detach ourselves from the mechanical outlook of the last century, which partially has been proved wrong, but which still burdens the field. Another example is the apparent misconception, which became the basic law of all science, that whatever we discover on earth is readily applicable to the whole universe. I intend to prove later that quite the contrary is true. Such laws today block our real understanding, and in time, after a fight, they will disappear, but they won't give up easily, because the stake is large—the souls of many misguided persons.

After that, let's take a quick glance, a bird's-eye view, at these basic sciences. It is not my intention to give a detailed summary of these subjects, but to point out their shortcomings, to show how uncertain our knowledge really is. Knowledge, or science, actually requires more faith than religion, and it still can't provide us with a solid foundation that could replace religious truth.

PHYSICS

Physics can be considered to be the most exact science. It deals with solid, touchable matter in great detail by setting up repeatable experiments, and by describing the results in the clear language of mathematics. Thus anybody can check the results of physics. It is as solid as earth. Still, physics has declared itself not to be an exact science, by introducing the uncertainty principle into physical results. The essence of this history-making discovery in physics is the confession that we are unable to perfect an exact instrument to produce exact measurements. All our laws are approximations, giving us more or less average results. Furthermore, physicists confess that it is meaningless to inquire about exact values, because all values are subject to uncertainty. For example, the exact size of an atom cannot be measured because an atom has no exact size.

Every experiment in physics is subject to this uncertainty principle. Imagine how the uncertainty principle affects other sciences that are confessedly not so "precise" as physics!

Physics today can be divided into three periods of development: classical, modern, and contemporary. The classical period developed the basic ideas of mechanics (the movement of solid objects), thermodynamics (the effects of heat), electromagnetism (the discovery and description of that phenomenon), optics (the nature and effect of light), hydrodynamics (the laws governing the flow of fluids), and the laws of ideal gases. Physicists by the end of the last century thought that their science was complete, that there were no more things to be discovered.

Then came the discovery of radioactivity, which opened up the realm of the atom. Following that, relativity forced physicists to reexamine our concepts of space and time, and later still, quantum theory was formulated to describe the inner working of the atom. Thus moden physics was born.

The discovery of the fission of the atom and of elementary particles not found naturally in atoms gave rise to contemporary physics.

Modern physics showed us that everything, including our physical body, is made up of tiny building blocks called atoms. But atoms proved to be further divisible, constructing an entirely new realm, the microcosmos.

The name "atom" came from the Greeks, and it means "indivisible." They knew that matter was built up from tiny particles, but they didn't know that even these tiny elements or building blocks of matter were still further divisible. Modern atomic physics showed us that an atom is a very strange thing. The size of an atom is very small, so small that we are unable to observe atoms directly, not even with the most powerful electron microscope. All we know about atoms is the result of indirect experiments measuring the effects they create. Most of these experiments involve creating catastrophic situations for the atoms. We bombard them, tear them apart, and then try to imagine what happened, while measuring the effect of the particles created by the experiment. This opens the question: Is our knowledge the true reflection of the conditions prevailing under normal circumstances?

There are two other things to consider. First, while we try to examine single atoms, in nature single atoms seldom can be found. Atoms are only members of large groups; most of the time millions, or more precisely billions, of the same or similar atoms act together. Thus single atoms virtually do not exist, except in the emptiness of interstellar space. Second, our knowledge concerns only the particular state of matter encountered on earth. Later I will discuss this in more detail.

Let us sum up, in a few words, what we know about the realm of atoms. An atom is built up of electrons and a central core called the nucleus. The size of an atom is approximately 10^{-8} cm. (This figure means seven zeros after the decimal point, followed by a one.) The size of the nucleus is a lot smaller than that. It is 10^{-14} cm. This means that the nucleus is a million times smaller than the atom. To imagine the difference, one should imagine a large football stadium as the fuzzy boundary of an atom, and in the middle of the field would be the nucleus, about the size of a pea. Thus we can conclude that as there is space in the football field, so there are vast, empty spaces inside an atom.

The nucleus is surrounded by electrons. The atomic structure was first imagined as being similar to our solar system. In the middle, like the sun, was imagined the nucleus, and around it orbited the elctrons, like the planets. Today this model has been partially abandoned and, on the basis of quantum mechanics, we imagine the electrons as energy shells surrounding the nucleus.

Breaking up the nucleus produced two kinds of particles called protons and neutrons. Later it was discovered that the neutron itself broke up into a proton and an electron, thus there is not that much difference between them. First, it was imagined that these two building blocks of the nucleus existed side by side as tiny spheres bound together by strong nuclear forces. Today, the energy shell theory prevails in connection with the nucleus, too. Since we gather our information from the nucleus by breaking it up, the possibility exists that it forms one unit, which differs only in size in the atoms of different elements, and only when broken up does it form the smaller units. But no such explanation has yet been examined.

All the mass of the atom is concentrated in the nucleus. The electrons are very small compared with it. As we know, there are many different atoms, with different qualities. The nature of an atom depends on the number of protons and neutrons in the nucleus. The smallest atom known is hydrogen. It contains only one proton and one electron. There are more than 250 known atoms with very different qualities. All of them can be made by multiplication of the hydrogen atom.

It was discovered that certain oversized atoms tend to disintegrate into two smaller atoms, emitting radiation. This is radioactivity. In certain atoms, such as uranium and plutonium, the disintegration can be speeded up under certain circumstances. If a critical amount of uranium is gathered together in chemically pure form, the slow fission of atoms starts a chain reaction, and a tremendous amount of energy is released in the form of heat and other kinds of radiation. This is the atomic bomb. We all know the devastating effect of the first two small, cruel atomic bombs in the fate of Hiroshima and Nagasaki.

However, the speed of the chain reaction can be regulated, and large amounts of useful energy can thus be gained. Nuclear power plants operate on this principle.

The opposite of fission is fusion. It was soon discovered that we can build atoms of a heavier element (that is, one with a larger nucleus and more atomic particles) from two atoms of a lighter one. The smallest atom, hydrogen, proved to be the easiest to use, building the next element in the periodic table, helium. The problem was how to unite two hydrogen atoms into one helium atom. To do this, we had to overcome a very strong force repelling the two nuclei. From theoretical studies, it was determined that a temperature of around 10 million degrees is necessary to ignite this thermonuclear reaction. Such a high temperature exists only in the center of an exploding uranium or plutonium bomb. The experiment proved successful, and the hydrogen bomb was invented.

Where does the tremendous amount of energy that occurs in both fission and fusion come from? When the two hydrogen atoms unite to form a new helium atom, the newly formed atom is slightly lighter than the two starting ones. The mass difference must be the source of the energy. But how can such a small difference account for such a huge amount of energy?

The answer had been found by Einstein, who established the relationship between matter and energy in the famous equation:

$$E = mc^2$$

where E is the energy, m is the mass of the matter, and c is the speed of light. This formula tells us that in figuring the conversion of a certain quantity of energy into matter, we can obtain the amount of matter that will result by dividing the amount of energy by the square of the speed of light, 300,000 kilometers per second (to "square" a number, or raise it to the second power, means to multiply it by itself). Conversely, when matter becomes energy, the amount of matter multiplied by the square of the speed of light gives the amount of energy that results. Thus we can understand that the conversion of such an infinitesimal amount of matter results in such a huge amount of energy because to obtain the amount of energy released in such a process, every amount of matter has to be multiplied by 90 billion, or 9×10^{10}.

I believe that Einstein's formula, especially the process by which energy becomes matter, is not yet completely understood. I will return to this later.

Today scientists are trying to tame the hydrogen bomb to produce a useful and abundant source of energy. At this moment the thermonuclear reaction has only one application: destruction.

Most of the energy released in this reaction appears in the form of heat. But what is heat? We still can't answer this question. The old kinetic theory of heat, based on the outdated mechanical view of the last century, examines the phenomenon only through its effects. Recently, physicists have become aware of this shortcoming, and have started to reexamine the theories of thermodynamics.

Heat must play a very important role in the process by which energy becomes matter. The discovery of a new phenomenon, the so-called fourth, or plasma, state of matter, clearly points in that direction. If we start to heat a solid substance, the solid becomes liquid. With further heating, the liquid becomes gas. These three—solid, liquid, and gas—are the three "normal" states of matter, those familiar to us in everyday life. With further heating of the gas, the molecular gas starts to dissociate into its component atoms. If the temperature increases still further, a very strange phenomenon takes place: the atomic structure starts to disintegrate. Electrons are stripped off from the nucleus, and at a certain temperature the gas becomes a mixture of freely moving electrons and nuclei. This ionized substance is the plasma state of matter.

On earth we know only the first three states of matter, but in the universe the plasma state is the most common. The matter in the stars is in plasma state, and so is interstellar matter. Thus we can conclude that the plasma state is the normal state of matter in the universe, and that *the states of matter we know on earth are only a rare exception*. The planets in the solar system account for only one percent of the total mass of the system. Even if we suppose that all stars have a similar planetary system, which is not the case, then matter in the nonplasma state accounts for only one percent of all the matter in the universe. To further complicate the question, we don't know in what state matter exists in the interior of the planets. Finally, we can conclude that matter as we know it on earth must be only a fraction of one percent of all the matter in the universe. This is why I think it is hopelessly naive to conclude that the laws of matter learned on earth are applicable to the universe. Thus, the first basic law of science is false, for all our knowledge and theories are based on experiments with this exceptional state of matter. We know that even the first three states of matter obey different laws, but we still want to apply these laws to entirely different states of matter throughout the rest of the universe.

This became evident to me as I studied the mathematical formulation of theories dealing with plasma. During the mathematical formulation of plasma physics, theoretical physicists found that heat and magnetism, the two most significant aspects of the phenomenon, fell out of the formulas, or, in other words, had no significance at all. Something must have gone wrong if the most essential feature of the phenomenon could not show up in the logic of mathematics.

The significance of plasma physics cannot yet be estimated. *Plasma physics could change our entire concept of the universe,* and in addition it could provide us with an unlimited source of energy. If we can tame the thermonuclear reaction of the hydrogen bomb, there won't be an energy shortage anymore. But this is a very hard task, basically because of the extremely high temperatures involved. No ordinary matter would be able to contain temperatures of 10 to 100 million degrees. The only possible confinement of such hot matter is within electromagnetic fields generated by giant magnets. Technical progress, however, can be made without a precise understanding of the inner workings of a phenomenon; thus it may be possible to succeed eventually in using the fusion reaction to generate useful energy.

The uncovering of many laws of nature by physics is the basis of our technology. These laws express numerical relations between basic phenomena. They do not necessarily mean that we understand the phenomenon itself. Such is the case with electricity. We know almost every aspect and application of electricity, but we still don't know what it is. We know it must be a phenomenon connected with atomic structure and energy flow in the outer part of the atom, and we have many working theories that provide more or less satisfactory explanations, but we still don't know just why such processes take place.

There are many questions still awaiting answers in this most precise science, physics, which is possibly the most thoroughly researched field of science, since it is so closely related to politics and the manufacturing of weapons. Countless billions of dollars have gone into weapons research, especially into atomic research to invent and perfect atomic weapons. Huge instruments like cyclotrons have been built, and legions of scientists have worked and still are working on such projects to hasten our destiny. Other sciences not related to this effort are poor beggars compared with physics, and yet even in physics we still have more questions than answers.

Even theories that have advanced into the status of laws are plagued with unanswered questions; for example, gravity, one of the oldest, most basic laws of physics, is constantly questioned. Many great men, including Einstein, have tried to find a way to incorporate it into a general energy field or force. Gravity can't be found in the microcosmos, and there are controversial theories that attempt to account for that fact. Some say gravity is caused by a still unknown particle called a "graviton"; others try to approach it as some sort of summarization of the individual electromagnetic fields of the atoms. I myself am inclined to believe in this last explanation. It makes sense that gravity would come from the individual atoms, and its neutrality would be the result of the summarization of the individual electromagnetic fields pointing in different directions, thus neutralizing the effect of each other inside an atom.

Quantum mechanics, with its uncertainty principle, confesses our inability to observe or uncover the true laws of the microcosmos. But it still allows us to formulate some workable formulas, based on empirical evidence, for use in technology. While physics has learned something about atoms by destroying them, the broken particles do not necessarily reflect the true nature of the whole, unbroken atoms. This may be the cause of our inability to incorporate in a system the particles, the result of the breakup. These particles simply defy our understanding.

Atoms are always acting together; thus individual treatment of them is meaningless. When we attempt to understand how they act together, we encounter a vast problem, the so-called many-body problem. The interaction of two spherical bodies can be satisfactorily solved, but when we add a third body to the system, we are stuck. The mathematical solution becomes extremely complicated, so much so that even the most powerful computer is puzzled. The problem becomes unsolvable if more than three bodies are encountered. But the interaction of many bodies is the basis of all phenomena in the universe! From the atoms to the stars, everything exists in spherical bodies, which interact and affect each others' movement and life. We are not exaggerating if we say that maybe the existence of the world is based on this, the interaction of many bodies, and yet we don't know how to approach it, not even in the most simple cases. Where, then, is our vastly overestimated knowledge? How can one put his faith on such a shaky foundation?

All our conceptions of the microcosmos rely heavily on motion, because the breakup of the atoms requires and produces speeding particles. Motion has become the basic idea of physics; everything is viewed as motion. But nature is harmonious, and though motion is important, I believe it is overemphasized as a remnant of the mechanical view.

All our theories are the products of some sort of philosophy, colored by individual taste and preference in the rating of facts as either important or unimportant. The official philosophy of science in our days is professedly atheism. The fact that some great scientists like Einstein or Heisenberg in their late years gave some thought to the existence of God doesn't really alter that statement. This philosophical basis can alter our knowledge considerably by ignoring facts that point toward God, and by preferring materialistic explanations. Speaking about God is considered unscientific.

As we have seen, the most precise science, physics, admits that we are very far from exact knowledge. Thus the best-researched science can't offer us any fixed point or solid foundation for denying a higher order above us. We have come a long way from Aristotle, who regarded earth, air, fire, and water to be the four basic substances of the universe, but we still have to admit that our knowledge is very limited. There are lots more problems to be solved than those we have solved with more or less success. Our knowledge has vastly improved, but we are still very far from understanding the universe around us. And any scientist who refuses to admit this is not a scientist at all!

CHEMISTRY

We have just taken a quick glance at physics, and we have learned that the basic building blocks of nature are atoms. We have learned that vast empty spaces exist inside the atom, and that the mass of the atom is concentrated in the nucleus. We have also learned that the mass is equivalent to a certain amount of energy, and that we can conceive of matter as condensed energy.

While physics deals with the single atom and its structure, chemistry examines the associations of atoms called molecules. Single atoms seldom can be found in our surroundings. Most atoms associate, if not with atoms of some other element or elements, then with other atoms like themselves to form pairs. Most commonly, in the earthly environment, different types of atoms are associated in different compounds. The best-known compound is water, in which two hydrogen atoms associate with one oxygen atom. The compounds making up rocks or even common dust are much more complicated than water. In them many atoms form marvelous crystal structures, which, under a microscope, display beauty beyond our comprehension. Some clear, overgrown crystals are the gems that are among the most valued treasures of men, such as diamonds, rubies, and sapphires.

It took mankind a long time to think of a way of ordering the atoms. First, it was necessary to analyze compounds into their component substance—substances that, because they could not be broken down into other substances, chemists knew must be made up of atoms of a single type. These substances were called elements; for example, the compound water can be analyzed as being made up of the two elements hydrogen and oxygen. On the basis of such characteristics as weight, in the last century chemists succeeded in establishing an ordering of the elements, called the periodic table. The newly established periodic table displayed the elements in orderly progression, with the exception of some gaps; subsequently, more elements were discovered to fill in these apparent gaps. The periodic table, in turn, was instrumental in the discovery of atomic structure by physics. It turned out that the smallest atom, hydrogen, is the basis of all other elements. All other atoms can be imagined as multiplications of the hydrogen atom. Today we know about 257 different elements, thus 257 different types of atoms.

There are countless possible associations of atoms, called

molecules. The chemical association of atoms in molecules does not affect the structure of the atoms participating in the compound. It affects only the outer electron shells; most of the time the outer electrons form a common electron shell around the two or more nuclei of the component atoms. Thus the atoms possibly become more stable within a certain temperature range. This brings us to a new aspect of chemistry, the application of the principles of plasma physics to it.

The association of atoms in chemical compounds exists only in a very narrow temperature range, one of a couple of hundred degrees. If we establish a scale ranging from the temperature of atoms on the surface of the stars, which is several millions of degrees, to absolute zero, called $0°K.$, chemical compounds can be found only near the lower edge of this scale. Above them is the realm of plasma; below their temperature range, the characteristics of matter also change, displaying such phenomena as superconductivity; finally, it is believed that at a temperature of absolute zero the structure of the atoms disappears, and possibly matter becomes formless energy again.

Above or below the temperature range in which chemical molecules exist, the association of atoms is unstable or does not exist. As we will see, this temperature interval is even narrower for living matter. Any theory that fails to incorporate the dependence of matter on temperature is at best incomplete. Thus we should understand that our surroundings on earth are indeed a rare phenomenon in the universe; less than one percent of the universe exists in such a form.

Chemistry is divided into two parts: inorganic chemistry and organic chemistry. Inorganic chemistry deals with the compounds that build up earth, while organic chemistry takes as its subject the countless variations of carbon molecules formed mostly with hydrogen. The peculiarity of these molecules is that they are the building blocks of living matter.

One of the chemical reactions that have the greatest effect on our lives is oxidation. This is the essence of fire, and it is the most common energy-generating method known to us, although the least effective. Despite this, it is the basis of our technology, even the most advanced technology, space research. In oxidation, some substance that has a greater affinity for oxygen than the elements associated with it, or "married" to it, in a given compound breaks up this previous marriage and forms a stronger bond with oxygen, while a small amount of energy is radiated in the form of heat. Actually, when elements exchange places in oxidation, a low-temperature form of the plasma state is occurring.

Since the discovery of the basic laws of chemistry, we have been able to add many new variations of associations of atoms to the vast number that can be found in nature. In our days we have surrounded ourselves with artificially created chemicals, and life as we know it now couldn't be imagined without them. This, of course, is not without side effects. We will deal with these newly created problems in Chapter 9.

It wouldn't serve my purpose to go any deeper into chemistry. Instead, let's take a quick glance at biology, the science dealing with the above-mentioned carbon molecules, which have a very special quality—namely, those molecules that carry the most peculiar quality of matter, life.

BIOLOGY

I pointed out earlier that the known chemical elements exist only in a certain temperature range. At temperatures above or below a certain limit, their characteristics change drastically. This temperature dependence is even stronger for organic matter. In most cases, the temperature band within which organic matter can exist is very narrow, the tolerance hardly exceeding 20 to 50 degrees.

Organic matter, the countless variations on the combination of carbon atoms with hydrogen, is part of the greater chemical environment of the earth, yet it is as different from inorganic matter as if the two represented different worlds. All living organisms are built up from a few elements besides carbon and hydrogen and exist as a watery substance. Water is the main ingredient of all living things, accounting for 50 to 90 percent of their weight. The rest of the weight is mostly carbon, hydrogen, and minerals, mainly calcium, accounting for the skeleton. The other elements, present in minute quantities, account for only a tiny percentage, and their importance is not yet fully understood. The body of man, for example, is about 78 percent water.

There are about one million different kinds of living creatures in the animal kingdom, and there are about a quarter of a million different plants. All are built up from the same carbon and hydrogen.

Biology started with the description and classification of living things. Gradually, the essential inner parts of the living organism were discovered. It was established that the common building block of all living creatures is the cell. The cell contains most of the essential features of the living organism. The most simple forms of life are composed of only one cell. Among the one-celled creatures we can find both plants and animals. The difference between them is that the plant cell can manufacture new products from the surrounding nonliving material using energy, while the animal cannot. In order to survive, the animal must take the manufactured product of the plant; in other words, it is the consumer of the plant. On a higher level, we find animals that can't even take the manufactured goods of plants, and must eat plant-eating animals to survive.

If we view this from the point of view of energy, the plant is the primary user of energy, the plant-eating animal is its secondary user, and the predatory animal is the tertiary user of the initial energy.

All functions significant to a living creature can be found in a single cell in the most primitive form. A cell is composed of a central nucleus, surrounded by watery cytoplasm. In the nucleus is a nerve center that coordinates the activity of the cell. There are primitive digestive systems to receive and to make use of an energy carrier; there is some sort of respiratory system to provide energy release using oxygen; the released energy is transported evenly throughout the cell; and waste is removed.

All organisms have the same systems, in more or less complex manners. In complex organisms composed of many cells, all basic functions are carried out by specialized cells, each of which performs only one task. It is as if many cells had consciously formed an association, dividing up the tasks among them, giving up their individual freedom, and becoming small, insignificant parts of a greater whole.

As we said earlier, only plants can manufacture organic material from inorganic matter. Each tiny cell that has this ability is a well-equipped chemical laboratory, surpassing the most modern man-made ones. But since there are animals which can't do the same but must use what the plants make, the danger exists that the animals can exterminate the plants if their numbers grow unchecked. To keep the balance, there are predatory animals, which control the number of plant eaters so that the plants will not perish. Man in our days has upset this balance of nature, which could lead to a very dangerous situation.

The most significant difference between living and nonliving material is that the living material is in continual interchange with its surroundings, without considerable alteration of its properties, and is able to reproduce itself.

In biology two new approaches were developed in the not-so-distant past. These two are biochemistry and biophysics. They open up the possibility of a new look at biology, to determine how much we really know about living matter.

Biochemistry tries to simplify biology into a summary of chemical reactions. A countless number of chemical reactions goes on in each living organism. Some of the simplest of these are more or less understood, but we are very far from understanding how these reactions are coordinated, how they affect each other, why a certain reaction and no other takes place, and how, exactly, cells are organized so that only one particular reaction takes place, and that only in due time. We are getting closer to understanding the role of the complex individual organs, but we are very far from understanding how the whole organism works.

As we saw, chemistry describes the relationship of individual atoms within a certain temperature range; in other words, it deals with many atoms interacting as large units. While physics tries to understand the structure of the individual atom and how it works, chemistry deals with the groupings of atoms. We are not yet able to understand the chemistry of the living matter, and understanding it in physical terms is one of the most hopeless tasks mankind has ever undertaken. Nevertheless, biophysics was born.

Biophysics tries to understand in physical terms the working of living matter. In spite of countless odds, it has produced some startling results, and it has opened up the path to a deeper understanding of our inability to know what God created, although this is not advertised or even talked about.

The most startling result of biophysics is the theory of the structure of the DNA molecule, believed to be the basic building block of the living organism. The controversial new science of bioengineering is based on this discovery. By splitting and rebuilding DNA molecules, new organisms, bacteria and viruses, can be manufactured. These new organisms often carry useful new characteristics; for example, the best-known are capable of eating up oil spills, and others are capable of manufacturing medicines. The controversy arises from the fact that in this way very harmful viruses and bacteria can be built, which in the hands of irresponsible persons or by accident can go out of control, thus causing uncontrollable damage and danger to all life on earth. There is another possibility: advanced bioengineering might be able to alter the genes of humans, thus producing people to do only specific tasks, robbing them of their freedom and personality, and realizing a world like that envisioned by Aldous Huxley in his famous novel, *Brave New World*.

Even in the smallest units of matter we are dealing with a great number of atoms. It is estimated that a single DNA molecule is built up of about one million atoms. The atoms form a spiral structure, very long, in three dimensions. One of the most prominent features of this molecule is that it is constantly checking itself by means of a unit composed of a relatively small number of atoms. This unit constantly goes around the molecule and checks to make sure everything is in order. If it encounters any irregularity, such as intrusion by a virus or a breakup of the molecule, it immediately cuts off the intruder, repairs the broken piece, or forms new parts so that the molecule will always be in perfect shape. No such process is observed in nonliving materials, for example, in highly organized crystal structures. Why does such unusual activity take place in the living molecule? Is there a special set of laws still unknown to us that governs the living organism?

In the "dark" Middle Ages it was believed that some special laws governed living matter. At the base of these laws was what was called the vital principle. But the atheists of the last century, instead of doing further research on this, discredited the whole idea of a vital principle. Not only was this basic understanding of life discredited, it was ridiculed. Earlier scientists simply denied the existence of a vital principle, and they did so without proof and without replacing it with another concept. The effects of this poor judgment linger in scientific circles even today, preventing a real understanding of life.

As we learned in our examination of physics, no usable mathematical formula exists for dealing with the interaction of many three-dimensional spherical shapes. Imagine, if we had such a formula, in the case of the DNA molecule it would have to account for the interaction of a million spherical atoms, lined up in a thin linear spiral structure in three dimensions, with some peculiar abilities, such as repairing and reproducing itself. And this is only one molecule!

Let us stretch our fantasy a bit more, and imagine a cell as it would appear if we could see the atoms in it. We could see many large molecules in the center of the cell, the nucleus, comprised of billions of atoms. Around it in the cytoplasm the number of atoms would be fewer, but would still be quite large. Between the atoms, according to physics, is a distance at least twice the diameter of the atom itself, and, as we know, there are vast empty spaces inside the atom. The picture that we can make for ourself is very similar to the picture of the galaxy. It is hard to say just how many atoms are in a cell (I don't have any exact number or accepted estimate, and perhaps no such estimate exists), but one can guess that the number of atoms must be a couple of billion. To extend the comparison to a galaxy, I believe that the number of stars in the galaxy does not surpass the number of atoms in a cell. The number of stars in a galaxy is estimated to be about a couple billion, also. The similarity goes further: usually the stars are concentrated in the middle of the galaxy, as molecules are in the nucleus, with the number of stars decreasing toward the edges.

It is estimated that the human body contains 60 billion cells (6×10^{10}). If a cell contains about a billion atoms, we can multiply that number by one billion to get 6×10^{13}, or a number with an initial 6 followed by 13 zeros. What a vast number! I would like to see a computer that could apply the principles of quantum mechanics to such a system, and give some explanation of how it works.

We can ask many more questions.

Why did atoms commonly encountered on the earth suddenly decide to form such a magnificent system? How can it be that this system is constantly picking up energy from the surroundings and putting it to work to move, to perform tasks, and eventually to reflect the universe like a mirror? How can two small cells reproduce the whole magnificent system in minute detail? Why does this system disintegrate after a relatively short time? Why did such a system come into being in the first place?

We can continue this line of questioning for a long time, but even these few questions can tell us how small is our knowledge. One more question is appropriate: *Where is thy knowledge, oh man?*

We are so proud of our knowledge, and yet, if someone asks the right questions, we ought to realize that we have not even scratched the surface of the knowledge that built and so wisely governs the universe.

If we were able to see nature as the collection of individual atoms, we would see a very strange picture. The ground would be composed of tiny stars with vast distances between them, bound together into a rigid, unmoving surface. Above it the density would decrease and the movement increase, with patches of fog-like creatures moving in the wind. These would be the men and animals, among them standing patches of fog, the houses and trees. But our eyes are not capable of seeing things this way. We see only the surfaces that reflect light. Depending on what they absorb, we see colors. The absorption, on the other hand, depends on the oscillations of the atom. If the oscillations change, we won't be able to see the thing. It is possible that we are unable to detect things existing beside us because of the nature of our eyes. And yet we don't believe in something we can't see!

Actually, science requires more faith than religion.

In light of this reasoning, isn't it hopelessly naive to suppose that a system as magnificent as the human body could be the result of accident? To suppose that there are no recognizable laws specifically governing living organisms? I believe there must be different laws that specifically regulate living matter and differentiate it from the nonliving. And there must be someone who placed these laws into dead matter to form the magnificent variety of plants and animals. Those laws probably include the laws of physics, but they must be vastly more complicated, and not only precise, but exact! The chance of our ever understanding the crudest one of them is very remote.

In this light, even our medical knowledge is just a groping in the dark, like a blind man trying to find his way. All efforts to prolong life are in vain and can result only in disappointment.

To sum up this chapter, we can say that, thanks to the uncovering (not discovering) of the realm of the microcosmos and a few laws that govern it—which we apply only to destroy ourselves—we are able to understand that we know nothing about ourselves or our surroundings. What we know is a very tiny fraction of the sea of knowledge, a cup of water compared to the ocean. We should not be proud of our knowledge; instead, we must be humble before the Creator of all this, recognizing our nothingness before Him Who not only knows the laws of all, but Who created them.

3

OUR KNOWLEDGE ABOUT THE UNIVERSE: ASTRONOMY

In the previous chapter we saw how uncertain is our knowledge of ourselves and our immediate surroundings. This uncertainty exists despite the fact that we can examine the things around us. We can touch, sense, weigh, and even take apart the objects within our reach to discover their hidden secrets and the laws governing their existence, and still our knowledge is very limited. We must admit that what we don't know is much greater than what we have learned.

The uncertainties plaguing our knowledge of the touchable world grow by powers of ten when we leave the solid ground of earth (mostly only in our thoughts) and try to understand the realm of the stars, the universe around us. One can compare the efforts of an astronomer to a man born in prison who has a cell with a small window, even this window covered by a curtain, who tries to map and describe the world with all of its wonders. He has an impossible task, doesn't he?

Astronomy has a bit more freedom, but it has very few facts indeed, and the rest is mostly fantasy. We apply the laws of physics, gained in the laboratory from experiments on a peculiar state of matter, to the entirely different universe. The knowledge gained in the laboratory, uncertain as it is, is extrapolated to cosmic phenomena. The legitimacy of this is highly questionable, even if we neglect the different state of matter that exists in the stars. It is a fact that theories built on classical mechanics succeeded in explaining most phenomena in the universe, and this should tell us something. Even if a certain set of theories seems to give a proper explanation, those theories still could be entirely false!

Following the basic discoveries of physics, all the newly discovered laws were applied to the whole universe. The history of these theories is very revealing, for the theories of yesterday seem ridiculous today. One example is the first explanation of how the heat of the sun is generated. It was assumed that the heat of the sun came from meteorites that wandered too close to the sun, were captured by its gravitation, and were crushed into its solid surface, and that the kinetic energy of this process was transformed into heat. This now-ridiculous belief was held quite seriously, and the believers in it would probably have fought with anyone who dared to oppose their "truth." The mechanical explanation of the universe was also thought to be so "perfect" that its disciples successfully convinced many that religion is only fairy tales. But eventually they were proved wrong when the more refined observations of this century revealed many new phenomena for which simpler mechanical theories couldn't account.

The discovery of radioactivity opened up a new way of explaining many phenomena in the universe. There was no significant delay between the discovery of fission and that of fusion. Fission was applied to geology to explain the heat flux from the earth's interior, and fusion was more successfully applied to explain energy generation in the stars, as it still is today. Will this also be outdated later? The answer must be an emphatic yes!

We have not yet arrived at the application of quantum mechanics to cosmic phenomena. Tremendous efforts are under way in our time to apply plasma physics to the universe, but many questions plague these efforts. Today's plasma physics is a mixture of classical mechanics (the emphasis is on motion and collision) and electromagnetism, which also carries a large burden of classical mechanics. Any revolutionary change can be expected only after the problems troubling theories of thermodynamics are solved.

H. Alfven, the renowned astrophysicist, introduced electromagnetism into astrophysics, but his efforts have not yet been fully understood and applied. Today the mysterious gravitation is still a ready-made explanation for all phenomena mostly because electromagnetism would complicate the picture behind our comprehension.

Today the tools of astronomy have been vastly improved, and more improvement is expected from space research, when we will be able to pull the curtain of the atmosphere by placing a telescope in space aboard a satellite. The telescope, the original tool of astronomy, is still the major means of gathering information. The information-gathering effort was improved by the radiotelescope and by the application of spectroscopy. All information that we gather comes to us in the form of light, which sometimes has traveled through vast, and for us meaningless, distances, through different force fields and interstellar gas and dust, which may affect or alter it. Centuries ago it was established that the force field of the sun alters the path of light as it passes by the sun, but such effects are regarded as negligible in modern science.

It was held for a long time that a special medium, the ether, occupied interstellar space, and that light traveled with the help of this medium. Recently this theory is fading away, but it is not yet entirely dead. However, in attempts to account for the way light travels, astronomical thinking has never dealt with the fact that a force field must exist between stars. If we think about the field between two stars, let us say the gravitational field, the gravitation decreases by the inverse square of the radius as we move from one star toward the other until we reach a line where the effect of the first star becomes zero. Passing this line toward the other star, we begin to feel an increasing pull from the second star. Weak as it is, this field is still the strongest force in that segment of the space, since no matter how weak a force is, it is the strongest if no stronger can be found nearby. The problem gets more complex if we add more stars into the picture, and finally we arrive at the unsolvable problem of physics, the manybody problem. This force field between stars has to be the special medium for traveling light. But since it is uneven, its effect on the traveling light is unknown.

The most solid ground in astronomy is the knowledge that we have gathered from our solar system. Even this modest knowledge has changed drastically in recent years as a result of space research using man-made satellites. After the data gathered by these satellites have been properly evaluated, most of our books on astronomy will have to be rewritten.

The first clash between religion and science is grounded in astronomy. It occurred when Kepler discovered that our earth is not the center of the universe. The old Greek model of Ptolemy, adopted by Christian theology, collapsed and gave birth to science. The discovery seemed unimportant at a time when astronomy was used only to correct or verify the calendar, but it later became the cornerstone of the new Tower of Babel called science, which has caused the enslavement and death of many souls.

Kepler's new theory turned out to be true. The sun is the center of our system, and the earth is only the third of the planets revolving around it. The sun has nine planets. The closest to it is Mercury, then come Venus, Earth, Mars, Jupiter, Saturn, Uranus, Neptune, and the outermost, Pluto. Pluto lately changed its orbit and now is orbiting between Uranus and Neptune. The first four, including Earth, are relatively small planets, while the rest, except Pluto, are giants. There are huge distances between the planets, but some regularity can be seen in the distances. The small planets are about 50 million kilometers apart, while the distances between the giants approximately double with each planet farther out from the sun.

We know a lot about the planets, but we have more unanswered questions than positive knowledge. Moreover, some of our knowledge has proved to be wrong; for example we imagined the planets as having extremely low temperatures of about -150° C. This approximation was based on the theory of "black body" radiation, which is still the basis of our temperature determination for stars and other objects in the universe. It has turned out, however, that instead of being extremely cold, the giant planets are very hot, sometimes as hot as a hundred thousand degrees.

The giant planets have many satellites, or moons. Some of them are almost as big as Earth. The pictures that Viking spacecraft have sent back are excellent, revealing many details of these strange worlds. Some of them consist of ice and rocks; others have active volcanos on the surface.

It turned out that the sun is not the center of the universe any more than the earth is. We are part of a gigantic star city, in which our sun is only an insignificant, ailing star; this star city is called the Milky Way. The latest estimate is that the Milky Way galaxy contains about two hundred billion stars. There are vast distances between stars. The nearest star to us, Alpha Centauri, is about four light years away. It is hard to imagine such a distance. During a blink of the eye, light travels around the earth seven times, and even at this speed it has to travel four whole years to reach the nearest star. If we imagine the sun as a one-inch ball, the nearest star is five hundred miles away from it. If that star were to explode at this moment, we wouldn't know anything about it until four years had passed, and the light reached us. But this is only the nearest star; today we talk about stars millions and billions of light years away from us.

We measure the distances to the closest stars by triangulation. This means that we measure the angle of the star from the two opposite points on the earth's orbit. This is called the heliocentric parallax. The difference between the values of these measurements is so small that, especially in the case of greater distances, the result is pregnant with error. It is believed that this method is fairly accurate up to about 300 light years' distance. Distances beyond this are estimates based on many factors, such as the brightness of the star and its spectroscopic picture. Variable stars are regarded as good indicators of distance, but all this adds up to the fact that our statements about the distances between the stars are only estimates, educated guesses if you prefer. For example, we know that the brightness of a star can depend on many factors. We may assume that a faint star is very far from us, but a bright, distant star would look the same as a close, faint one.

Much of our information about the make-up of the stars comes from spectroscopy. In spectroscopy, white light is broken up by a prism to show the colors of the rainbow, the spectrum. If the light travels through a gaseous material cooler than the source of light, a pattern of dark lines will appear in the spectrum. Light radiated by different elements also shows lines at different places. Thus the spectrum can be utilized to tell us many things about the source of light. The fact that while traveling through immense time and spaces the light can encounter many modifying phenomena is recognized only in our days. During the writing of this book astronomers reported an astounding finding. A distant quasar records its presence in a double image. Its image split by the warping of its light through the gravitational lens of a massive galaxy about midway between the quasar and earth; thus we record two stars instead of one. This account of an optical illusion on a cosmic scale is only one example how shaky really our knowledge is about the universe.

There is another interesting phenomenon connected with the spectrum. If the spectrum of the star is moved toward the red end of the scale, it is believed that the star is speeding away from us. This is called the red shift. Lately, however, the validity of this theory has been questioned.

Our galaxy can be compared with distant galaxies to get some idea of its shape. It is believed that the Milky Way looks very like the Andromeda Galaxy. At the center of the galaxy is a brilliant region, with an estimated diameter of twenty thousand light years. About fifteen thousand light years from the center is the first spiral arm. There are four more arms, about six thousand light years apart. The last one is very faint, and it lies about forty thousand light years from the central region.

It is believed that our galaxy is only part of a larger supergalaxy, which has a diameter of 40 to 50 billion light years. But this is mostly speculation.

We have gathered a very large body of observations, but we have no means of verifying the accuracy of these observations. This doesn't keep us from making theories to explain them, and nothing is wrong with that. The wrong starts when we forget that our explanations are only theories or hypotheses and start to believe in them as if they were truth, and, on the basis of that "truth," claim that no other truth can exist.

We have interesting hypotheses about the life of the stars, their inner structures, and how they and the universe formed. Let's take a quick glance at them.

Today scientists imagine that the stars consist of more or less dense, gaseous material. It is supposed that the main ingredient of a star is hydrogen. In the center of the star this hydrogen feeds a fusion reaction, which provides the star with energy. Sir Arthur Eddington is the current authority on the interior of stars. He has set up a mathematical description of the inner workings of a star. Gravitational pressure is supposed to keep the fusion reaction in line, preventing it from becoming an H-bomb by a chain reaction, but how it works no one knows. Most astronomers consider Eddington's thoughts to be revelations, to be received with proper reverence. However, many mathematical models of a star's interior were devised previously, and all proved inadequate under the pressure of accumulating observational evidence. I believe something is wrong when mathematics advances into judgeship instead of serving as a tool for thought. Today Eddington's thoughts reign over astronomy, and since astronomy can't be checked by experiment, it is inevitable that authority alone decides what is to be believed, what is acceptable, and what is not.

The fact is that we know nothing about the interior of the stars. The best studied and closest star to us is the sun, and even its surface provides us with so many puzzles that no single theory can possibly account for all of them.

Stars are strange objects. One of their most peculiar features is their density. It was found (let's not question how) that the density of stars has an amazingly wide range. Some of them, such as Betelgeuse, a red giant star, have a density less than that of the vacuums that can be artificially created on Earth. New studies have shown that the density of many young stars differs only slightly from that of the surrounding empty space. On the other hand, there are very dense stars, called white dwarfs, composed of material a thousand times heavier than lead. The companion of Sirius is one of these ultraheavy stars. Our star, the sun, has a density about the same as that of water. The giant planets are similar. It is interesting, however, that the small, inner planets are a lot denser than the sun. The densest of them is Earth, which is 5.5 times denser than the sun.

In our days stars are believed to be born and die, just like people. This notion came from the observation that there are giant stars whose diameters are sometimes greater than that of the whole solar system. These stars are believed to be very young. Some of them are blue giants, which seem to be throwing energy into space like crazy millionaires who have more than enough of everything. However, the density of these stars is hardly distinguishable from that of empty space. These stars are believed to be youngsters, born only a few million years ago. Many of these young stars can be found in groups, called clusters, consisting only of similar young stars. They are believed to be speeding away from their birthplace in all directions. Then there are the red giants, representing the next step in development. They are a lot more cautious with energy. According to present theory, they have already burned up their hydrogen entirely, and they consist only of helium and heavier elements. On the surface of these red giants, spectral analysis sometimes reveals very complex, heavy elements. In comparison, our sun is believed to be a middle-aged gentleman, and the oldest stars are believed to be the heavy white dwarfs. They die as supernovas, leaving in their place only a huge cloud of dust and gas.

Many theories try to explain how our solar system originated. All of them are based on gravitation, and no theory can be proved or disproved, since the solar system originated long ago, and either no similar process can be observed among the stars today, or the process differs so much from what we imagine that we can't recognize it even when we do encounter it.

The first of the many theories is the Kant-Laplace nebular hypothesis. Kant and Laplace argued that the sun at one time was surrounded by an atmosphere that extended beyond the present limits of the solar system. Then the sun contracted by gravitation, and the surrounding nebula formed rings and finally planets. This theory was introduced at the time of the French Revolution. It had an incalculable effect upon the scientific, philosophic, and religious thought of the nineteenth century.

Another well-known theory, called the tidal theory, was introduced by Sir James Jeans. This theory supposes that the solar system came into existence by chance, when a wandering star came too close to the sun and pulled material out of it, roughly in the shape of a cigar. The cigar later broke up into planets.

The current theory (in my view the most illogical) is that the sun and the planets were formed at the same time from a cloud of dust. The sun was formed from the central region of the cloud, whereas the planets came into existence from the outer part of it.

None of these theories pays any attention to the theories of stellar evolution. If a star is born, as it is believed, as a blue giant, with a diameter greater than the diameter of the whole solar system, and die as a white dwarf, where in this evolutionary scale can we find a place for our sun and its planets? There is also the problem of density. Would it not be more plausible to suppose that at a given time in the life of a star it would give birth to planets as a natural stage in its life? But the present theory of the structure of the stars excludes such a possibility.

Astronomy provides a perfect example of the way politicians of science imagine science must work. In observatories the astronomers, like busy bees, collect data, and then cosmologists fabricate theories from it. The astronomers are the scientific workers; the cosmologists are the licensed thinkers. Don't ask who gives out those licenses, or why, or when! Cosmologists are the chief priests of astronomy. Of course they won't stop at the edge of the solar system in fabricating their theories; they want to seem to know how the universe itself originated!

The current theory of the origin of the universe is the "Big Bang" theory. It is a masterpiece of fantasy, which accounts for the origin of the infinite universe with its countless number of galaxies filling infinite space. This theory presupposes the existence of a huge amount of energy in the form of thermal radiation. This thermal radiation, during the first five minutes of the existence of the universe, changed into matter, into the simplest form of it, of course, protons and neutrons. During the next half hour more complex matter was formed, like deuterium and helium. Then the reaction got tired, so to speak, and we must wait about 250 million years (why not more or less?) for the next action. At that time the hydrogen-helium cloud started to break up into protogalaxies. Then again no action took place until a thousand million years had passed, when the galaxies suddenly condensed into stars and planets, and the universe was ready to accommodate us.

If you dare to ask why only thirty minutes was needed for the huge amount of energy to become matter all over the infinite universe, the cosmologists are ready with an answer: the explosion of the atomic bomb took only about one microsecond. But they forget that the comparison is basically wrong. The state of the universe was entirely different then. Neither the temperature nor the state of matter can be compared. The situation of the two is light years apart; moreover, they are comparing fission with fusion.

But why should we have such an explanation? Why should all the energy convert into matter during the first half hour? It took me years to arrive at a solution to these questions, after finding a more logical solution to the basic question of how the universe originated. But let's discuss it in the next chapter.

4

NEW PERSPECTIVES IN ASTRONOMY: THE DEATH OF MATERIALISM

In the previous chapter we took a quick glance at astronomy. We saw that despite the enormous body of observations we have gathered, thanks to expensive and vastly improved instruments, our knowledge still is very imperfect. Most of our "facts" turn out to be estimates, all of them plagued with uncertainties a thousand or sometimes a million times greater than those of physics. But if you read a popular scientific book on astronomy, you may never be aware of those uncertainties. In such books, educated guesses are presented as irrefutable facts! The reason is clear. The authors want you to believe in science, to put your faith in those "facts." In reality, science requires more faith than any other religion. Those who put their faith in science believe in men instead of in God, a God whom many in our days find not a worthy object of study.

Just how shaky our knowledge of the universe is cannot be better illustrated than by the new discoveries of space research about our immediate neighbors in the solar system. Our knowledge of them should be the greatest, since they are almost within our reach. Our theories were greatly detailed, but the satellites proved our imaginations wrong, and all our books on those bodies had to be rewritten.

I was trained as a geologist, but unfortunately for me I was "cursed" with an inquiring mind. Life for me was full of "why's" and why's can be the source of many troubles. Since my early youth, when communist schools first introduced me to the theory of Darwin, instead of accepting the "new truth" as most of the others did, my mind was bent on solving the conflict between religion and science, at least for my private use. An impossible task, I know now, because there is no conflict between science and God! But there is a grave conflict between the politics of science and God!

When I finished my study in the university, my interest turned to the questions of historical geology. I saw many conflicting ideas in geology just waiting to be solved. As I advanced in this study, it became more and more clear to me that no solution is possible unless someone can come up with an appropriate theory about the origin of the solar system. The many conflicting theories now existing side by side range from an icy cold origin to a hot origin for the planets. There is a great conflict between these theories and the theories of stellar evolution.

I came to believe that the formation of planets must be an organic part of a star's life. It can't be a rare occasion, caused by accident or chance, nor can it be part of a star's formation, because this contradicts everything we observe about young stars. Therefore I turned my attention to the sun, since the sun is the only star we can study, and unless we understand the sun, we can know nothing about other stars.

If one considers the history of outdated hypotheses about the sun and the stars that were once believed to be firm theories (the history of science usually is carefully avoided in textbooks to prevent possible skepticism about recent hypotheses), one easily can understand Alfven's statement that all our theories are just enormous extrapolations of newly discovered physical laws. In the light of his statement, our present theory of the structure and interior of the sun is nothing but the enormous magnification of an H-bomb. But the hydrogen in the H-bomb is very rapidly converted into helium in a chain reaction. What keeps the hydrogen in the interior of the sun from doing the same? It is simple, say the cosmologists: the pressure of gravitation does. But how? No one seems to know. Physics tells us that a hot plasma can be confined only by very strong electromagnetic fields, but no such field appears in the current explanation, only neutral gravitation does, and yet we don't even know how gravitation acts inside a sphere!

This hypothesis about the interior of the sun comes from Sir Arthur Eddington. His authority on that matter is not to be questioned; even in serious publications I have many times seen it called "unquestionable." But whence this authority comes still puzzles me.

When I examined the sun, sun spots came to my attention. These are the only windows on the sun's atmosphere, the only opportunities to look below its surface. Then I was shocked. The bottom of the sun spots is black. But if the source of all energy, including light, is located in the center of the sun, why aren't these openings the brightest part of the whole surface? Why are they black instead? The only possible answer to this riddle is that the source of energy is not in the center of the sun. But then where is it, and just what *is* in the center of the sun?

Then I wondered about the density of young stars. Their density if almost identical with that of the surrounding space. They have almost no weight. From physics we know that all matter has weight, but some very small particles like the photon do not, and energy is also weightless. If all the stars, even their insides, consist of matter, this should not be the case. They should have definite weight. The only possible solution can be that the interior of the stars consists of the original energy. Since the energy is weightless and has no density in the material sense, the interior of the star has to come from the material on the surface, which encloses the energy like a shell, confining and protecting it from energy-poor space. The sun spots are tears in this shell; they are holes, discontinuities created by the disturbances of magnetic fields.

I'll never forget the moment when I first looked at the sun with this new understanding. The face of the sun was covered with light clouds, acting like smoked glass, so that I was able to see it. Then I realized that it is only a huge bubble of energy confined within a shell of gaseous matter. I stood spellbound with the magnificence of the moment, knowing that I was the first to see the sun this way, and that I had gotten a bit closer to understanding the greatness of God and the tininess of myself. This was in 1967.

The possibilities of publishing my discovery in communist Hungary were very limited, and I felt I badly needed to do further research on the subject. Since then I redoubled my effort to leave the country. Finally I succeeded, in 1971, and in 1972 I stepped onto the free soil of America. After the initial difficulties of a stranger in a strange land, finally I got the opportunity to do some private research in the New York Public Library. I reviewed hundreds of books and articles, and my conviction that I was right grew stronger day by day.

In 1973 I formulated my idea and published it in a tiny booklet. I mailed it to about a hundred eminent publishing astronomers, asking them to respond with criticism, or in any form. I was green and overenthusiastic. Not one single answer reached me.

In writing this book, I read my booklet once more. I have to admit it wasn't perfect. There were language errors in it, and it may not have been as clear and scientific as something like that should be. Still, I think, despite its errors, it should have moved the imagination of any open-minded scientist.

Thinking about the failure of my pamphlet made me realize that I had violated many unwritten laws governing today's scientific world. First of all, I hadn't earned the right to speak up. Instead of digging a small hole by earning a Ph.D., I declared myself a thinker, not a scientific worker, claiming for myself a position reserved for those who have previously proved that they will comply with the politics of science and its governing philosophy: materialism and atheism. My age did not permit me to go up the ladder step by step and defy science from the top, so I had to give up.

But you just can't get rid of an idea so deeply seated in the mind. I couldn't cease searching for new evidence. In January 1976 the newspapers carried a sensational article about a new discovery in astronomy. The discovery was the observed periodic pulsation of the sun. The observation was made, independently, by two groups of scientists, one in Russia and the other in the United States. The conclusion that both teams drew from the phenomenon can be viewed as direct evidence proving my hypothesis.

The Russian team seems more bold in its conclusions. A.B. Severny and V.A. Kotov in their article, "Observation of Solar Pulsation" *(Nature*, January 15, 1976), stated that the time of the pulsation could be explained if the sun were taken to be a homogeneous sphere. (This would exclude the possibility of a central energy-generating mechanism.) Furthermore, they concluded that the proton-proton reaction alone could not be the source of all energy radiated out from the sun, because if it was, the energy output, the luminosity of the sun, would be ten thousand times less than its observed value. The sun then would be unable to supply the energy needed for life on earth.

The American team—J.R. Brookes, G.R. Issak, and H.B. Van der Remy— in their article in the same issue of *Nature* didn't dare to go so far in their conclusions. However, they mentioned very cautiously the possibility that the interior of the sun may be pure energy, although they immediately backed away from this thought and instead mentioned the possibility that the interior of the sun might be a black hole. (The black hole is a mysterious phenomenon with unusual properties; one of its most significant properties is that not even light can escape from it.)

If I am right and the interior of the sun and other stars still consists of the initial energy of the universe, then a lot of mysteries of current astronomy can be solved. My hypothesis does not differ radically from current theories, and observations seem to support it all the way. The whole hypothesis is based on Einstein's formula:

$$E = mc^2$$

This formula, in my opinion, is a description of how energy becomes matter. But, as we saw in plasma physics, the structure of matter is dependent on temperature. We are still waiting for a proper explanation of just what temperature is—it may be the amount of freely flowing energy in a system— but until someone comes up with a proper explanation, we must be content with the old name *temperature*. Matter in Einstein's formula must be a function of temperature, even if the importance of temperature is negligible when energy becomes matter. While fission is independent of temperature, the opposite, fusion, is highly temperature-dependent. Therefore, I believe Einstein's formula has to be modified:

$$E = m(\mathrm{f}T) \times c^2$$

where matter *(m)* is a function of temperature. Why the speed of light *(c)* plays such an important role in the formula can be explained only by the dual nature of light. It is at one time a wave of energy and the smallest particle of matter, called the photon; thus it can be seen as the transition between energy and matter.

If we conceive of the formula as a process, and of this process as taking place in the boundary between the energy inside a star and the gaseous material forming its shell, we should find young stars with shells of very thin material. In fact, a few stars that have been photographed have such a thin material on their surfaces that the contour of the star can be seen only as rings, inside which the stars behind shine through without obstruction.

We can now explain why the density of young stars is so low. They have only a thin film of hydrogen on their surface; the rest is weightless energy. This way even the strange phenomenon of pulsars can be explained. As matter grows on the surface of the young star, it becomes a red giant. In the cooler, outer part of its atmosphere, the possibility opens for heavier elements to form. This is exactly what we can observe.

After a longer period the shell of the red giant becomes thermally unstable, as A.V. Sweigart summarized in "Evolution of Red Giant Stars" in *Physics Today* (Vol. 29).

Since a large percentage of the universe consists of binary stars, I believe the next step in the life of a red giant is the formation of a binary system. The thick shell of matter, obeying some as yet unknown laws, is torn off from the star, and, since the spherical form is predominant in the universe, from the atoms to the stars, I believe it immediately forms a sphere from the gaseous matter and becomes a proto-planet. The interaction of the two results in smaller planets in a gradual process of development. I will discuss this in more detail in Chapter 6.

My hypothesis can also explain the origin of the universe. The new explanation accepts the basis of the big bang theory, that in the beginning there was a large amount of energy. Was it in the form of thermal radiation? I believe it wasn't, because thermal radiation is only one manifestation of energy. But what is energy? The answer should be: we don't know! Any serious thinker has to admit that while we know many forms of energy, we don't know what energy is. Furthermore, we don't even have a hope of learning just what energy is. We have failed to learn what is the energy content of an atom, although we know it is condensed energy, and our chances of learning the energy of the interior of the stars are a lot less than for the atoms. The properties and laws governing these huge chunks of energy confined in the interior of the stars are sealed from our knowledge. They are, for us, unknowable. But if the greater part of the universe is sealed off from our searching minds, then the proud statement of materialism that nothing in the universe is unknowable is basically wrong. Our knowledge narrows down to explanations that account for less than one percent of the universe, and I have shown in previous chapters how imperfect our knowledge of even that small, knowable segment is. This can mean only one thing: materialism is false, misleading, a dead idea.

Now we can understand why it is necessary in a theory like the big bang for all the energy to convert into matter during the first half hour. It comes from the necessity of proving the false theory of materialism and its faithful companion, atheism.

Isn't it more logical to suppose that the initial amount of energy first broke up into large energy units, forming the protogalaxies? Then, slowly, on the edges of these protogalaxies stars started to form. In the distances separating the protogalaxies, there first appeared light, the first representative of matter. Just as our Bible says, "And God said: 'Let there be light'; and there was light" (Genesis 1:3). Observation has proved that young galaxies are round, and stars can be observed only on their edges. The star-forming process gradually progresses toward the center, and, as we saw, even in an older galaxy like our Milky Way the energy density is greatest in the center regions. Our sun is a middle-aged, middle-sized star. Is there any connection between this and its place in the galaxy? As we know, our sun is located near the edge of the galaxy. The vast majority of observations seem to prove this hypothesis.

Is it possible that large chunks of energy in its original form still float inside the galaxies, gradually breaking up into stars? When Ambarcumjan, the Armenian (Soviet) astronomer, studied the young stars, he found that they are born in groups called clusters, and he open-mindedly questioned the present dust-cloud hypothesis as the only explanation for their birth. Can we identify these floating islands of energy with the mysterious black holes? I believe that that may be a logical conclusion. The fact that not even light can escape from them should mean that this energy acts like a solvent, making energy from matter. We could detect only matter reflecting or emitting light, not energy. This is why the interior of the sun is dark; it is neither emitting light nor reflecting it. If the sun suddenly lost its atmosphere, we would see only a black hole in its place.

How can the tremendous amount of energy the sun radiates be accounted for in the light of this new hypothesis?

As we saw, the proton-proton reaction alone is not sufficient to explain this energy. But from physics we know that the proton is a giant particle compared with the elementary particles. Among them, the smallest is the photon. Might not such particles as protons and neutrons be products of a gradual buildup? Lately a new theory to this effect, the kvark theory, has surfaced. It tries to reduce the number of particles to three initial particles, called kvarks, and all other particles are supposed to be multiplications of these three. If we start from energy, a gradual buildup of bigger and bigger particles seems quite plausible, and this process, like the proton-proton reaction, results in energy production. The process then continues with the building up of larger elements, but there must be a limit, a temperature limit, to the size of the elements that can be built upon the surface of a star. The size of the surface elements depends on the thickness of the material shell.

By now you may be able to see why such a theory is unacceptable. Despite its logic, strong support from observational evidence, and a clear superiority over current speculations, it is unacceptable. Why? It took me a couple of years to figure that out.

It is unacceptable and dangerous because it means the death of materialism and atheism, the basic ruling philosophies of science.

This hypothesis could be worked out in detail, but that is not a task for one person conducting private research; it would require teamwork. A review of the current literature, surprisingly, almost entirely supports with observational details this new set of theories. But can you imagine a university that would want such revolutionary change in current ways of thinking? Not even a Christian university would dare to dissent and to go against the prevailing currents in today's scientific world. Today, if an observation does not fit a theory, it is explained until it does fit.

Many open-minded astronomers are aware of the conflict between theories and observations. From time to time, many express their doubts. As two astronomers, J.N. Bahcall and R. Davis, put it in their article, "Solar Neutrinos: A Scientific Puzzle" in *Science* (January 1976), the conflict is so large and elementary that it must be due to an error in basic physics. I believe the conflict comes from the materialistic and atheist philosophy that has ruled science for centuries. This philosophy is like a straitjacket binding and suffocating scientific thought! Until science can free itself from this restraint, it will walk in the deepest darkness, although some scientific clown may boast that we have reached the peak of our knowledge.

5

EVOLUTION: A TRUTH OR A LIE?
INTRODUCTION TO DIMENSIONS

Is evolution a truth or a lie? I believe it is both. It is a lie embedded in truth: a most dangerous mixture, invented by the archenemy of God. The word itself is confusing. Its meanings include, first of all, all processes unfolding in time, but they also include progress or development, by which the evolutionist means that all process will result in time in a better, higher condition than when it started. This is contrary to the truth. Experience shows us that a process in time can go in both directions. To illustrate this with a paleontological example, let us consider the reptiles. The once-great reptiles, the largest of which were bigger than a one-story building, still live with us without major change, as tiny lizards. Their evolution resulted in just the opposite of progress.

The word *evolution* has become identified with the theory of Darwin, who used it to explain the origin of animal species. He said that all life forms on earth are the result of a long development in time by chance, by natural selection, and by the survival of the fittest in a constant battle for survival. By excluding God from creation, he created a dogma for the emerging new world religion, atheism. His dogma today is preached as true in every school on earth, including many religious ones. The identification of the word with Darwin's hypothesis is a perversion of its original meanings.

Before we analyze Darwin's hypothesis, let us consider the truth in the word *evolution.* To do this we have to examine our perception of dimensions.

We live in a three-dimensional world. Its dimensions are: length, breadth, and height. But do we always think in all three dimensions? The answer is no. The average man usually uses only two dimensions in his thinking. Not only the average man, but even most scientists think this way; for example, take diagrams, which are usually in two dimensions, and the many difficulties that arise when we try to make diagrams in three dimensions. Almost all our ideas are presented and perceived on two-dimensional paper. Of course, the situation is more complex than that, but we can safely say that most of our thinking neglects the third dimension.

The life of an average man revolves around home and workplace, virtually in two dimensions. We know very well that the shape of the earth is round and that it is floating in space, but essentially this is outside and foreign to our way of thinking. Only very few men imagine, for example, the events of the news on the three-dimensional globe, with all the peculiarities of the third dimension. This is similar to our perception of large sums of money. Many executives have to decide on the investment of millions or billions of dollars, though they can perceive only their pocket money or, at best, their salary. Similarly, the distances treated in astronomy mean nothing to most men.

The fact that we think only in two dimensions was a common and accepted way of life before the scientific revolution. The earth was imagined as flat, which was logical because everybody could see that it was flat. The introduction of the third dimension, together with the heliocentric view, shocked this well-established way of thinking. The whole building of ancient thought collapsed, and its falling walls indiscriminately also buried many treasures of ancient thoughts, among them the values of religion. But the earthquake caused by the heliocentric way of thinking didn't stop there. The discovery of immense space was followed by the discovery of great lengths of time. Time is today considered to be the fourth dimension.

The immense distances in time, or in the fourth dimension, further eroded ancient thought, and this shock still prevents our establishing a clear line of thinking. The matter is not yet settled, because of our inability to experience fully the third and fourth dimensions. Only a very few, specially trained men can really think in the fourth dimension; even their thought is basically two-dimensional and is burdened with many misconceptions, since we virtually do not exist in the fourth dimension, at least not in our present material form. Time is just as inconceivable for us as the distances in astronomy. But we have to accept those huge distances, because our observations have shown us that they are real. Even our nearest neighbors, like the moon or the planets Venus and Mars, are so far from us that such distances no longer mean too much to our senses. Similarly, we have to accept the fact that huge distances exist in time. We measure time by years. A year is only one round trip of our earth around the sun, our star. One round trip is so long for our perception that millions, or even billions of them seem to us like eternity. In that scale our life would be not even a dot, and even thousands of years would show up only as a point. This is why it is so hard for us to think in the fourth dimension, time.

In our attempts to conceive the reality of higher dimensions, mathematics can give us a helping hand. During the last century, Rhineman, one of the disciples of Gauss, the German "Prince of Mathematics," put the possibility of higher dimensions into mathematical form. Mathematics in our days is regarded as the perfect proof of reality. If a thought can be expressed in mathematical formulas, it is accepted as truth, as we saw with the recent theory of the structure of the sun. If we follow this line of thinking, we can safely say that the existence of higher dimensions is a proven fact, despite our inability to sense them.

In his theorem, Rhineman supposed that if two-dimensional beings existed, like bits of paper on a large, flat surface without volume, those beings would not be able to sense a three-dimensional object. For them such an object would not exist because their senses would not be able to perceive it. But if they were intelligent enough, physics and mathematics would say to them that higher dimensions must exist, because they would be able to handle mathematical problems in such inconceivable dimensions. Rhineman did not even try to limit the number of conceivable dimensions.

We are similar to those two-dimensional beings. Though we live in a three-dimensional world, as I stated before, most of our thinking doesn't leave the level of two dimensions. The only ones among mankind who have fully experienced the reality of the third dimension are the few astronauts who have visited the moon. They saw how small, actually, earth is, how insignificant all our earthly struggles, our daily pursuits, our hustle and bustle, our fights and our ideas are compared with the magnificence of space and the infinity of the universe.

Really to conceive or to experience the fourth dimension, time, is a completely hopeless task. We do not exist in that dimension. Our life is only a prolonged microsecond in that dimension. All our perceptions of time are guesswork, and not even those who work with millions of years can really conceive of its meaning. How, then, could a man perceive with his reason the higher dimensions? The possibility exists, that the fifth dimension is represented by energy.

In geology we try to estimate the age of the earth by using a few faint clues. We believe our guesses to be accurate, but there is no way to prove them. We suppose that the fission of radioactive elements was always the same and that they can be used as clocks, but we don't really know for sure what factors may have affected fission during the past many millions of years. Our other methods are equally uncertain; thus we can present a hypothesis, but we never will be able to prove it.

There is an example from the Bible of just how uncertain are our methods of determining time. At the dawn of this century there were many reports that Noah's Ark had been found. Some explorers even brought back with them pieces of petrified wood believed to be from the Ark. The wood was subjected to different methods of dating, and the results showed great variation. The method that uses radioactivity said the wood was about 150 thousand years old, while other methods confirmed the Bible, showing only 6,000 years. Which one was correct?

The uncertainty increases as we go further back in time. When we talk about millions or billions of years, the uncertainties must increase by millionsfold. Thus, speaking about knowledge of these periods just doesn't make sense. All our knowledge remains only hypothesis, or, in other words, the opinion of one or just a few men accepted by a few others and declared to be truth by authority. Such a truth requires more faith, faith in the opinion of man, than the most incredible dogma of any religion. Events may have happened in the way that a scientist imagines them, but they also may not have. We will never be able to know for sure.

As I mentioned earlier, the introduction of the third dimension resulted in the collapse of the old way of thinking. The discovery of the fourth dimension, time, further eroded the old values and was perceived as the final blow to theology, to all religious truth. Some clergymen even unconsciously helped this erosion by sharpening the question, saying that if the theories of science prove to be truth, then God does not exist. Such statements helped the growing skepticism about the truth of religion. The scientific theories in the long run prevailed, because they were based on perceivable reality, perceivable dimensions, while the religious truths are inconceivable by the reason of our mind, because they apply to higher dimensions. As the imaginary two-dimensional beings wouldn't be able to see or otherwise sense the reality of the third dimension, so we are unable to sense in any way the higher dimensions—but this doesn't mean that no such things exist. As we saw, mathematics is even able to prove their existence.

What was new in the discovery of the fourth dimension? Mostly the unusually huge distances in time, foreign to our everyday experience. Some scientists meditating on the meaning of time discovered that enormous changes had to have taken place during the history of the earth. Then proof arrived. Marine fauna was found on dry land, even on the tops of mountains, indicating that enormous changes in the shape of the earth had indeed taken place. The concept of evolution, of slow changes having enormous effects in the course of time, was introduced. Using the thickness of some strata, various calculations attempted to estimate the time that was needed to make up the huge amounts of sediments, and then came trouble. The calculated time in no way fitted into the time table that had been made up by some zealous theologians speculating on the first book of the Bible, Genesis.

Again the question was phrased in such a manner that, to the delight of atheists, it implied that either geology or the Bible was truth. The question really is: How valid were the speculations on the Bible? It turned out, unfortunately, that science was right and those speculations were wrong, and science went on to conquer the minds of men.

But there is no contradiction between the Bible and evolution. The Bible clearly states that the creation of the world took place in time. I believe that the story of creation, told us by Moses, is somehow only a crippled remnant of a once-real knowledge. In time the real knowledge somehow faded away and was possibly modified a bit throughout the passing ages before Moses put it into writing. For example, it doesn't make sense that light was created twice. The creation of light was the very first act of God, on the first day, but later we read that the sun and the moon were created only on the fourth day. Why? The puzzle never can be solved unless we accept the idea, proposed in the previous chapter, that from the initial energy, whatever it may be, God first created light as a transitional element between energy and matter. But the explanation will stop here and continue with the early history of earth.

During the past hundred years or so, many have tried to reconcile the story of Genesis with scientific hypothesis. Needless to say, all of them have failed. Why? Not because the Bible is wrong, but because our present knowledge is still far from being perfect, even from being settled.

Recent research in geology has projected a possible way of reconciling the two, but first many false ideas must fade away. Genesis says that at first the waters filled the earth; so does geology. First the water was in the air as steam. Later it condensed and covered the whole surface of the planet. The dry land appeared only later. Of living things, Genesis says that first the ocean was populated, and later the dry land, just as does geology. We know that the primeval atmosphere contained mostly carbon dioxide, covering the sky with huge clouds, which not even the sun's rays could penetrate, but that the carbon dioxide was converted into oxygen by vegetation. *This is why the sun and moon were "created" only on the fourth day, while light was created on the first.* This means that the sun and moon had appeared only on the fourth day but were created earlier. And we know that man was the last of the creation; so says science, too. What is the difference, then? Where is the contradiction between the Bible and science? The six days? Why? Who can say "I know how long a day is for God"? God does not exist in time! He must be above all dimensions!

But geology wasn't that advanced in the last century, thus no such comparison was possible. The atheist of the last century grabbed the opportunity of turning the results of the first primitive approaches in geology against the Bible and God. But their joy wasn't complete. If God didn't create the world, He certainly could not have created life, they thought. How, then, did life come into existence? And the endless speculation began. First, they were very careful. This was the time of the sowing of the idea that creation may not have been a divine act. Voltaire can claim the merit for this, since he ridiculed creation. But Darwin was needed to formulate, in *Origin of Species*, the second dogma of atheism, falsely identified with the word *evolution*. A.D. White, in his book *A History of the Warfare of Science with Theology in Christendom*, called Darwin the high priest of atheism, "The gentlest of mankind," who was savagely attacked by the reactionary clergy from all denominations.

Darwin's hypothesis is well known, for it is preached in schools all over the world today. Its essence is that God has nothing to do with the creation of life. Organic matter came into being by pure chance and slowly evolved into more complex living things through the process of natural selection based, of course, on sex preferences and through a ceaseless fight among all living things for survival. Only the fittest survive, while others, the weaklings, perish from the face of the earth. Lyell, the other hero of that age, gave Darwin a helping hand by hypothesizing a basic law of nature, the law of uniformity. This law is one of the false basic laws of geology. It assumed that only those forces and circumstances that can be observed today formed the surface of the earth. This theory excludes the possibility of sudden changes. It even supposes that temperature was always the same. All changes, it assumes, were the result of slow evolution, of weak forces acting through countless millions of years to result in the present face of the earth.

Recently Velikovsky picked up this glove and tried to prove how unfounded this hypothesis is. In his two books, *Worlds in Collision* and *Earth in Upheaval*, he documented hundreds of bits of evidence proving that the law of uniformity is unfounded and false. In hundreds of cases he showed that major catastrophes had taken place and had tremendously affected the face of the earth, the climate, and life itself. He tried to prove that such catastrophes had taken place even in the past few thousand years, and that they can even be traced in ancient myths and legends. These catastrophes not only refute Lyell's law of uniformity, but they can be viewed as arguments against slow evolution. Much evidence can be found that the theory of the survival of the fittest is wrong, since these catastrophes wiped out entire species that were otherwise well equipped to survive not only climate, but the attacks of enemies as well. The best example is the mammoth. This huge, elephantlike creature was very strong; it was equipped with fur to survive the chilling climate; and it was able to defend itself against its enemies. Still, it was wiped out without a trace, as the result of catastrophic changes.

Velikovsky was refuted, ridiculed, and eventually silenced, despite his "good will" in given a helping hand to atheism by explaining some miracles in the Bible as natural phenomena. The hypothesis of Darwin is considered sacrosanct in scientific circles today. Anyone who dares to express doubt about it is regarded as unfit to be called a scientist; not only that, such a person is regarded as unfit to hold public office. The media were very angry over Ronald Reagan's stand on evolution during the 1980 presidential election campaign. Today most of our scientific ideas are based on some form of evolution. It has become a dogma, like the existence of God in Christendom. If you doubt it, you doubt science, and this is a major sin in our upside-down world.

Let's assume for a moment that Darwinism is true, and that the different species evolved from each other. According to Darwin, this process required millions of years. If it is true, we should have countless proofs, transitional forms showing how this new god, chance, operated. There should not be any difficulty in finding abundant evidence everywhere.

Like busy bees, Darwin's disciples swarmed out to collect those transitional forms, but they found none. They turned every stone and still found none. The search for evidence of evolution, for the missing links, is excellently documented by A.N. Field in his book *The Evolution Hoax Exposed*. But if you think that such a failure to find evidence discouraged the atheistic believers in evolution, you are wrong. They fabricated a few, which were later exposed. Any sane man, seeing no evidence to support his thoughts, would give up—not so the Darwinists. The idea was so perfect, it suited so nicely their line of thinking, atheism—the collection of many lies—that one more lie didn't bother them at all. They decided that any opposition must be shouted down, and shout it down they did. They succeeded in intimidating all sorts of opposition. They got a big hand from all atheists, who slowly had taken over every important post in scientific life and quietly had weeded out everybody who dared to oppose materialism and atheism. Today Darwin's lies are taught to your sons and daughters as irrefutable truths.

Is there a seed of truth in evolution?

Common sense tells us there must be. According to the naive interpretation of Genesis, God created each animal species from clay using His humanlike hand like a man molding a sculpture. This is hopelessly primitive in the light of our present knowledge. A more complex explanation must exist.

As we saw, the universe that we can see is so huge that we are unable to explore it, even in thought. God, Who created the universe, must be still greater. The Being Who created the universe must have a special method of creating life. The creation of the universe and of earth itself, as the Bible tells us, unfolded in time. Though the Creator was ever present, we don't have to suppose that He made it with His hands.

The whole question of evolution boils down to this: Did God use inorganic matter to create each individual species? This hardly can be the truth, though with God nothing is impossible. As we saw, although on the atomic level inorganic matter differs only slightly from organic matter, the difference is still enormous. The atoms of organic matter must obey a different set of rules than inorganic matter does, otherwise the atoms of organic matter would remain in their perfect, inorganic state. Organic matter is so complicated on the atomic level that even a single cell is more complex than the galaxy. We know now that in a living organism the information, or program, for how to reproduce itself is written in the genes, which in turn are combinations of many DNA molecules.

Theoretically the programs of the molecules can be changed; thus new species can be formed by one who knows the meaning of the program. In nature we can find both simple organisms and complicated ones; the peak of them all is man.

The Bible unambiguously states that God took the material of our bodies from the inorganic matter of the earth, from the dust. This doesn't exclude the possibility that God gradually developed the inorganic matter of earth into organic matter, from the simple to the more complex. It is even possible that when He wanted to create a new species He used some of the existing species, rearranged the program in the DNA molecules, and the new species was born to the world. If the whole immense universe was created by His single wish, why can't we accept the fact that He didn't have to work with His hands? His wish actually was enough to accomplish the diversity of creation—so perfect, yet still so simple.

In this way we can keep all the important features of evolution in complete harmony with Genesis. The Bible tells us the creation went on in time. Each new step can be imagined as based on an existing one, but still as an individual creation. The one thing that we must deny is that it had anything to do with chance. Nothing was left to chance, or to evolution through transitional forms. We can safely state that this is true, since there is no evidence to support the hypothesis of transitional forms. New species seem to have come into being with extreme suddenness, complete with all the features that characterize them. This explanation excludes the necessity of catastrophe, also, though we have to admit that cosmic catastrophes must have taken place in the long history of the earth. Neither catastrophe nor slow change resulted in the diversity of life on earth. Creation undeniably bears the signs of a Creator, who made all things according to His plan, unknowable for us.

To try to understand an organism on the atomic level is a completely hopeless task. Just think about the complexity of our bodies. How can one imagine seriously—even for a moment—that this complex entity came into existence by sheer chance? Some computer scientists have meditated on this question and have tried to use powerful computers to answer it. They concluded that if only chance had operated, then life would still be on the level of viruses, thought to be the transition between living and nonliving matter.

Eventually, we have to arrive at the conclusion that lots of elements in Darwin's hypothesis can be regarded as truth. Unfortunately, this "gentlest of mankind" was an atheist, serving his master, the father of all deception, who is the master of mixing truth and lie. By his inspiration, Darwin equated God with chance to serve the purpose of atheism. But he failed hopelessly to show mankind a single piece of evidence, outside of some slight resemblances, of how this chance had worked in time.

A very sensitive question still remains to be answered: Did God use the primates to create man? What if He did? The resemblance between apes and men warrants a yes. But does this mean that man is the descendant of the apes? The answer must be a positive no! God only used—if He did—the material developed in the monkey, the dust of the earth made living by Him, to create a completely new species, the most complex of all: man. From the very first moment, the new creature was entirely different from the material used to create him. And he had a unique feature, his soul, which elevates him above the animals. Or casts him below them, as in some cases in our days.

As we saw, Darwin's theory is a strange mixture of truth and lies. It was made purposefully to deceive. If Darwin had believed in God, he would have made his theory support God, as a possible way of understanding God's way of creation. But we can safely assert that this wasn't his intention. He wanted to disprove the existence of God, wanted to give a strong weapon to atheists to use against God, to purposefully deceive many, even the elect, if that would be possible. He succeeded in every way. Even in his lifetime he was able to harvest the recognition and admiration of the world, which is governed by Satan. Another high priest of satanism, Marx, openly praised him, together with all the destructive spirits of the age.

The theory of the survival of the fittest soon gained social application, as justification for the predatory nature of early capitalism, the exploitation of workers, who were not even allowed to have the basic necessities of life. This in turn pushed them into the hands of communism, the worst form of modern slavery, created with the sole purpose of driving God out of the earth. The poison of this misconception saturates all aspects of our life. Darwinism is the basic dogma in communism. Soviet scientists have further developed it, describing how inorganic matter becomes organic. Their fairy tales in turn are taught to youth, poisoning their minds in the earliest stages.

6

GEOLOGY: THE KNOWLEDGE OF OUR PLANET EARTH

Geology is the subject most abused and misused by atheism against religion. It is a set of hypotheses based on examination of the surface of the earth. All our efforts to understand the earth can be compared to the efforts of an intelligent bacterium who happens to be on the surface of an egg and from there tries to figure out what could be inside, how the egg was made, and so on. This intelligent bacterium probably never would be aware of the hen who laid the egg, and we know that from the egg alone one might never figure out how it came into existence.

Our efforts in geology are similar; they are a very complicated process of guessing. A simplifying tendency is clearly visible in all our theories dealing with the subject of how the earth came into existence. Some even go so far as to try to apply Lyell's principle of uniformity, saying that the same forces that operate now, and only those, have operated throughout the long life of the earth, even before men appeared on its surface. This is dangerous, because it prevents free thinking aimed at working out more complex solutions that may be closer to the truth. It is customary to have a single hypothesis and to force the evidence to fit it, thus to explain a very complex system with only a single idea.

As we saw earlier, the matter known to us at the surface of the earth is anything but normal in the universe. It is a unique state of matter, near the lower edge of the temperature scale, and less than 1 percent of the universe exists in such a state. Ninety-nine percent of all known matter exists in the plasma state, which differs considerably from that of normal matter as we know it. This fact is not yet fully understood and utilized in our understanding of geology, especially not in our theories about the origin of the solar system.

Before we attempt to summarize the hypotheses concerning the origin of the earth and the solar system, let's take a quick glance at our egg, earth, and what we know about it.

As we know, our earth is the third planet of the solar system. It has an almost perfect spherical form, and its radius is about 6,371 kilometers. Its average density is about 5.5 grams per cubic centimeter, while the density of the surface rocks is only 2.8 grams per cubic centimeter; this means there must be an increase in density toward the earth's center. Various experiments indicate that the temperature also must incrase toward the center.

Less than 30 percent of the earth's surface is land; the rest is covered by oceans. Most of the land is concentrated in the northern hemisphere. The water in the polar regions exists in the form of snow and ice. We do not know whether the same division existed throughout the long history of the earth, or whether at one time sea and land existed in different proportions.

The land has many mountains, while the sea has many great valleys. The depth of some of those valleys exceeds the height of the highest mountains on land, though when compared to the radius of the earth, the differences are negligible.

The topmost layer of the earth is called the crust. Its thickness is uneven. Under the continents it varies from 30 to 60 kilometers, while under the oceans it is only 5 to 6 kilometers thick. The crust contains many sedimentary deposits, products of disintegrating rocks. Below this we can find the mantle. The mantle is relatively thick; its lower level is believed to be 2,900 kilometers deep. The remaining part of the earth is called the core. All these divisions are based only on changes in the velocity of seismic waves.

By attempting to interpret smaller velocity changes, geophysicists have divided both the mantle and the core into many more layers, interpreted as changes in the condition of the matter that built up the earth. Thus the core is also divided into two different parts. The inner core does not transmit seismic waves.

The earth shows some similarity to a blast furnace used to smelt iron. As the result of heating, the iron sinks to the bottom, while the residual rock floats to the top. This gave scientists the idea that the earth's core must consist of iron. The existing magnetism of the earth also strongly supports this idea, and many see the meteorites as further evidence. The iron and nickel meteorites falling from time to time on earth are believed to be part of an exploded planet's core. It is generally believed today that the present structure of the earth is the result of a process of development. There has been a lot of speculation about this development, but no proof is in sight, since the only data that we can have are the seismic waves.

The question of how the solar system originated has fascinated many great minds during the past few centuries. Sincere scientists admit that the question may never be solved scientifically, since almost all evidence that could be used to establish the validity of any hypothesis has vanished without a trace. The only thing one can do is attempt to derive the present state of the solar system from an assumed set of events occurring in the distant past.

Most hypotheses suppose that the solar system is the result of a single event occurring in a relatively short time, and most hypotheses are unable to harmonize with other theories like stellar evolution. They suppose the sun was always the same as we know it today in size, in energy output, and so on.

The line of hypotheses started with the great philosopher Kant, who in 1755 worked out a hypothesis of the origin of the solar system. His idea was later worked out mathematically by Laplace (1796), and it is known as the nebular hypothesis. I have to admit that this hypothesis has more logical features than any that has appeared since, including our presently accepted one. Kant supposed that the planets originated from the material of the sun. He supposed that the sun was a lot larger than now, and this is in agreement with the theory of stellar evolution. The sun must have been a giant in its younger years. Furthermore, he assumed that the sun consisted of gaseous matter, as is still held today, and that at a certain point this matter started to contract. By this contraction its rotation became more rapid, and gaseous matter was torn off from it.

The expelled matter formed rings, which later condensed into planets. No one since has been able to override the theory of a ring, or rings; it always resurfaces, but no one seems to know why.

Around the turn of the century this hypothesis was abandoned, and gave way to the so-called catastrophic theories. The most prominent representative of this sort of theory is J.H. Jeans. He supposed that the planets are the result of a cosmic catastrophe. A star passed by the sun, and its gravitational effect pulled out from the sun a cigar-shaped mass of matter that later broke up to form the planets.

A transitional theory surfaced around 1940. It is in some ways a return to the nebular hypothesis. The representatives of this theory assume that sometime in its life the sun went through a gaseous dust cloud like those observable as diffuse nebulas. By its gravitation, it gathered a large envelope around it, and this envelope later condensed into clouds, then into planets.

The currently accepted theory is very similar. The only difference is that the sun and the planets are supposed to have formed at the same time from a "gaseous dust" nebula.

The common feature of all these hypotheses is that they explain the origin of the solar system using purely mechanical forces such as gravitation, friction, and the collision of particles to produce heat and centrifugal force, though we know that gravitation is almost nonexistent on the atomic level, and that instead electromagnetic forces play a great role in determining the behavior of particles.

In the history of science, Alfven must take the credit for first breaking away from the conventional mechanical outlook and introducing new elements into astrophysics: magnetic and electrical forces. Research in our days has shown how important these forces are in astronomy. They may prove to be more important than gravitation. Modern research has shown that electromagnetism plays a very big role in the life of the sun and other stars and even in the life of the galaxy. The galaxy itself has a general magnetic field.

Alfven attempted to formulate a hypothesis about the origin of the solar system using the two new forces, magnetism and electricity. He started from the popular assumption, the foreign dust cloud. He supposed that the sun then ionized the cloud, which started to fall toward the sun because of gravitation. This fall was broken by strong magnetic fields, and planets started to form. One of the main objections to the acceptance of this hypothesis was the enormous value calculated for the necessary magnetic field, 300 thousand gauss, compared with the present measured average magnetic field of the sun, 2 to 3 gauss.

Though Alfven wasn't successful with his theory, or rather with the details, his approach to the problem is still the best. I believe his basic mistake was yielding to the then-fashionable foreign-gas-dust hypothesis.

It would be beyond the scope of this book to give a new, detailed hypothesis about the origin of the solar system, but since I have introduced a new model for the structure of the sun and stars, I feel obliged to give a sketch, at least, of how this new concept might affect possible solutions to the present problem.

I believe Kant was right when he suspected that the planets must have originated from the matter of the sun. They are her children, born in her early youth. Thus we have to follow the life of the sun if we want to solve the puzzle of how the earth was created. The sun must have been a blue giant after its birth. I believe the fact that the sun is positioned on the edge of the galaxy has played an important role in its life. If we accept the hypothesis that the galaxies evolved from a round shape to the most recent stage, the well-known spiral form, then the sun might have been born among the first stars when the Milky Way was still a lot richer in energy. This may mean that stars with planets can be found mostly around the outer edge of the galaxy.

As a young giant, the sun must have exceeded in diameter the present limit of the solar system. We have supposed that this young giant was a giant bubble of energy. On its surface, hydrogen was formed rapidly, while tremendous amounts of energy were thrown into space. If the Einstein formula is right, the tremendous amounts of energy are needed to form a single atom:

$$m = \frac{E}{c^2}$$

This must mean a contraction. But since we know nothing about the properties of the initial energy, we have to admit that we don't know how this process operates.

As the material on the surface grew, it must have put pressure on the enclosed energy. The enclosed energy had to have the ability to withstand this pressure, and among the properties of energy, electromagnetic forces must play an important role. From laboratory experiments we know that heating a plasma can be done by electromagnetic forces only, and confinement of the extremely hot plasma is possible only in an electromagnetic vessel. The opposite, some kind of attraction, must be true in the case of a star. Electromagnetic forces must attract matter to the surface. Or is this the result of gravitation? Or of all three together? It is very hard to answer this question. We know from observation that the sun spots, which I believe expose the enclosed energy, have much greater magnetic fields than the surface atmosphere. Sometimes these reach the order of several thousand gauss, and some binary stars have a magnetic field of 34,000 gauss.

The abnormality of the electromagnetic field in the sun results in sunspots and flares. In the flares, matter is ejected above the surface, sometimes over a couple of hundred thousand kilometers, but it falls back again, since it doesn't have enough energy to escape; at least no such phenomenon has been observed during the short period of regular observation. Theoretically, it is possible that such a mass might escape to form a smaller meteorite, and this raises the possibility that in the past such disturbances occurred on an immense scale.

Our young giant gradually became a red giant as the matter on its surface got thicker. At this phase, heavier elements appeared on the surface, as they can be observed in red giants today. At a given point, we have to suppose that an instability occurred, which must have been connected with electromagnetic forces. As a result of this instability a large mass of matter was ejected; the material shell of the star was peeled off. This may have been accompanied by a contraction. Although a large amount of matter was spread about, the bulk of the material immediately formed a large sphere. I believe there is a very strong force in the universe inhibiting scattering. Only a supernova explosion can overcome this force. We can observe this force at work in welding. When the hot iron or other metal particles fall freely, in a relatively short distance, before they get to the ground they form tiny spheres. We have to suppose that the same phenomenon occurs in space. Thus not a ring, as was assumed by Kant and later thinkers, but a huge ball of fire was formed.

This newborn star wasn't a star at all, since it had not free energy inside, but consisted of matter in the plasma state. It was a giant protoplanet. Beside it was the sun, a medium-sized, ultra-hot blue star again. Many such binary systems can be observed today. As a matter of fact, some astronomers say that most stars in the Milky Way are binary systems. As for the mechanism, the forces that acted at this birth, I believe it is as yet beyond our comprehension. We may expect some solution if plasma physics overcomes its initial difficulties. Neither mechanical nor electromagnetic forces are sufficient to explain beyond the shadow of a doubt what went on at this birth. Recently a strange star, SS 433, has excited astronomers. The phenomena observed at that star defy all known laws. Is it possible that we are witnessing the birth of a binary system?

Most binary stars have irregular orbits. One star is at the focal point of the ellipse, while the other revolves around it on an irregular elliptic orbit, at times close to the other, at times far from it. This could have been the case with the ancient binary solar system. As the new protoplanet cooled and contracted, instabilities may have occurred on its surface, and at the right moment, when it was near the sun, the sun could have pulled out large masses from it. I believe the higher elements of the periodic table were formed in the protoplanet, where the temperature was a lot cooler than on the surface of the sun, even at its red-giant period, although the plasma was still hot enough and turbulent enough for collisions of many medium-sized elements to form one greater one. Many larger elements do not produce energy when forming, but even take heat from their surroundings. The matter torn off from the protoplanet would immediately assume a spherical shape; thus a third planet would be formed. It is possible that the outer giant planets were formed first, and from them, in a more complicated interaction, the smaller planets and the satellites of the giants, which differ only slightly in size from the smaller, inner planets. Jupiter may be the remnant of the first protoplanet. As planets were formed, their orbits became more regular, as we know them now. Of course, this can be worked out in more detail, and could be modified a bit.

If we imagine the solar system as a giant electromagnet, as much evidence suggests, we may begin to understand why all of the planets rotate in the same direction. Even the irregularities in the axial rotation can be explained using the above-sketched mechanism, and we can say also why all planets occupy an orbit around the equator of the sun. No one ever saw the poles of the sun, but we know it is flattened around the poles. I think it is possible that this huge electromagnet has field lines similar to those we can observe when we place a paper over a magnet and throw iron particles on it. I believe the planets position themselves around the field lines about the equator, where neither the north nor the south pole attracts them. If this is true, distances can even be calculated using it. The question remains: How well do we know what is going on inside the magnetic field of a giant magnet, which is complicated by electric forces? As soon as the new planet was born, it would take up one of the possible orbits, marked by the field lines, and modify the whole system of orbits around the sun.

How a planet develops later must depend on its size, its orbital distance from the sun, and many other unknown factors. There must, however, be a size limit. Above this size the planet would be unstable and still capable of launching a satellite. The stability of the satellite also has to have definite criteria. Some satellites must be able to escape from the original orbit of the giant planet, to wander inside the system causing trouble, colliding with another satellite, or taking up an orbit. If that is possible, it could modify the orbits of the others as Velikovsky showed in his book: *Worlds in Collision*. Many factors that could have played an important role in the past will never occur again; thus we will never know what really happened.

We can assume that the earth was born in the same way. It must have been first a giant ball of plasma that contracted by cooling, compressing the plasma in the interior and thus storing tremendous amounts of energy. This energy, in the form of heat flux, still comes up to the surface extremely slowly and steadily. Some scientists still maintain that this heat flux is due to radioactivity. However, it was shown scientifically that their theory is simply not true. Laszlo Egyed, a geophysicist calculating the occurrence of radioactive elements, has shown that even if the earth contains in its deeper regions as many radioactive elements as on the surface (which is not true), even this much radioactivity could not account for the heat flux from the interior. But this assumption is still widely held. Egyed doesn't mention the plasma. He calls it degenerate matter, which is extremely compressed. But I believe the term *plasma* is more appropriate.

With the cooling of the surface, normal matter as we know it appeared, and gradually went through the phase transition, forming the solid crust. The transition zone between normal matter and plasma can be seen today as the boundary between the mantle and the core at a depth of 2,900 kilometers. It must be the result of a gradual cooling. While at first contraction occurred, later the earth started to expand. In the plasma the atoms are stripped of their electrons or have deficient electrons around the nucleus; thus they can occupy less space. The cooling and the transformation into normal atoms coincide with the completion of the electron shell, and thus cause an expansion that in turn results in the expansion of the earth. It is believed that the earth's original surface before the expansion began was only what we now know as the continents. The expansion resulted in the surface occupied at present by the oceans.

When the surface was cool enough, the waters condensed. This began at the temperature of 360° C. The waters covered the whole surface of the small earth, and only later, when the expansion made it possible, the dry land appeared. This is in complete harmony with Genesis, which describes this as the gathering of the waters on the third day. But Genesis connects the appearance of dry land with the creation of vegetation.

This is logical if we suppose that in the seas some protolife, some one-celled animals, existed, and that from them God created vegetation. The higher sea life was created later. The link between vegetation and the appearance of the sun and moon can be proved. The primeval atmosphere, before the vegetation changed it, contained mainly carbon dioxide and large amounts of water vapor. It was a lot thicker than what we know now. An easy estimate can be made if we calculate the carbon dioxide equivalent of the known coal reserves of the earth plus the carbon dioxide bound in limestones and dolomites. The change of the carbon dioxide in the atmosphere may have resulted in the chemical separation of the limestones and dolomites from the oceans. The age of those carboniferous materials—sedimentary rocks—seems to prove this assumption. This separation also affected the possibility of the appearance of higher sea life in the less salty waters. This change in the atmosphere made it possible for the sun, which wasn't visible through the thick, opaque atmosphere, to appear first in the sky on the fourth day. The sea was first populated with life, as paleontological evidence shows, in harmony with Genesis, on the fifth day; then the earth was populated on the sixth.

The appearance of vegetation made possible, first in large, shallow marshes, the appearance of dry-land animals—the primitive cold-blooded reptiles. They found abundant food and could grow to enormous size.

Organic life, together with the gradual cooling, had a tremendous effect on the development, or evolution, of the earth. I made a detailed study of these two effects in 1968, but I wasn't able to publish it in this highly specialized world of science. I was told that I would have to cut it up into small pieces and bring it out gradually, but for me that didn't make sense. In that study I estimated that the earth's temperature was about 35-40° C at the beginning of the Mesozoic era. This temperature gradually dropped to a value of 4-5° C during the estimated 130 million years at the beginning of the next era, called the Cenozoic era, which began 70 million years ago, if our methods of determining time are correct. This cooling resulted in the possibility of the appearance of the warm-blooded animals and their gradual takeover of the earth from the reptiles. Although the large amount of carbon dioxide maintained a greenhouse effect, as it was used up by the vegetation this effect diminished, and with that the vegetation changed to the species that we know today.

No one seems to be aware of the importance of the earth's own temperature in its life. Today the earth's surface temperature is attributed solely to the sun's heating effect, but this is only partially true. The surface temperature of the earth is the sum of two components: the sun's heating effect and the earth's own surface temperature, which is the result of the steady heat flux coming up from its interior.

The earth's own temperature at its surface can be identified with the temperature of the deep sea water. The oceans cover 70 percent of the earth's surface; consequently they must exhibit the basic temperature of the surface without the effect of outside factors, particularly in places where the sun's heating effect is negligible. In a more detailed study, some fine effects must also be taken into consideration, but for an estimate we can safely say that the basic surface temperature is between -1 and -4° C, or on the absolute scale of temperature, on the Kelvin scale where the freezing point of water is 273° K, it is 272° K. Let's assume, for the sake of simplicity, that the difference between winter and summer months in America is about 30° K, the span 273° to 303°. If the earth's own temperature would be 0° K, the heating effect of the sun would be only 30° K, instead of 303° K. Thus we can see how important an effect the earth's own temperature must have on its surface. I believe this temperature was a lot higher during the long period of the history of the earth, and it cooled gradually to the value we have now.

The decreasing temperature at the beginning of the Cenozoic era created a situation that was unfavorable for the cold-blooded reptiles and made possible the creation of warm-blooded animals, and eventually men.

When the temperature got below 4° C on the poles, ice and snow appeared for the first time in the history of the earth. By freezing large chunks of water—it is estimated that if the polar ice were to melt, the level of the oceans would rise 30 feet, or 10 meters—the uneven distribution of this heavy load may possibly have caused the poles to wander. I believe Velikovsky was right in attributing the extensive ice cover in the ice age to the wandering of the poles, rather than to extensive cooling over a larger region of the earth and a warming later.

No such process can be justified but it is still widely held, regardless of its weak points.

Some geologists insist that the primeval atmosphere of the earth dissipated at an early stage, and the present atmosphere is the result of vulcanism. But if we accept the hypothesis that the earth's core is highly compressed plasma, and that the phase transition was gradual and is still under way, then we also have to suppose that when the plasma was a lot closer to the surface, it created a strong electromagnetic force that, together with gravitation, was able to hold the primeval atmosphere.

If we accept the plasma hypothesis about the earth's core, we may have an easy solution for the origin of the earth's magnetism and electricity. The origin of the earth's magnetism is currently a controversial, unsolved problem. Many models have been devised to explain its origin, but none of them is convincing enough to be widely accepted. Presently the dynamo theory is the only accepted explanation. This supposes that the core of the earth rotates at a different speed than the mantle, and that this creates a dynamo, which causes the magnetism and the electrical phenomena of the earth. But this is just a compromise solution, and its mechanism is hardly imaginable.

On the other hand, plasma has its own electromagnetic field. The individual ionized atoms and electrons, if they are oriented in the same direction, could make up a giant dynamo. If the earth's core is matter in the plasma state, we may use the laws of plasma physics to understand better how the earth's electromagnetism originated. This plasma hypothesis, though, doesn't exclude the possibility that the core is rich in iron. This hypothesis can also provide us with the proper explanation of the steady heat flow to the surface. The plasma hypothesis may be suitable to explain why some planets have magnetic fields around them, and others don't. I believe that in those planets without magnetic fields, the original plasma has already undergone the phase transformation, and only magma is found in their cores.

As we saw, the development, or evolution, of the earth is in complete harmony with the Bible. As a matter of fact, the Bible can provide explanations for things science has not yet been able to account for. For example, as I wrote this chapter I recognized that Genesis must be right, and indeed the vegetation must have appeared before the sun and moon, because it was needed to catalyze the change in the atmosphere. This made it possible for the dissolved limestones and dolomites to settle out of the sea in order to let appear the higher life forms in the sea on the fifth day, and on the sixth the land animals.

When we try to unfold the secrets of the long history of earth, we are just guessing, step by step, how omnipotent God created it. Studying it with a humble spirit, we recognize the grandeur of His work. In contrast, studying it to disprove His presence, as atheistic, worldly science does, results in misunderstanding and chaos.

It is marvelous to see how simple the universe is. Everything is built up from energy bubbles, as huge as stars or as tiny as atoms, but is nonetheless the energy that proceeded from the mouth of God when He decided to create, and said, "Let it be." Everything around us is built up from this energy; functions and appearances differ, but the substance is the same. We can also understand why our world is only the shadow of reality if we accept the fact that reality exists in the higher dimensions where a part of us, our soul, really belongs.

We can see how wrong materialism is when it restricts our thinking to this level of reality, and deprives us of even the search for the higher levels, saying that the search is useless nonsense. God and our soul exist in higher dimensions that we are not even able to comprehend. They are far beyond the possibility of experience by our limited ability in this material body, but they still exist, as we would exist even if two-dimensional beings could not conceive of the level of our existence.

Most knowledge is nothing other than the opinion of one man, accepted by many, but still a man's opinion. Whoever puts his trust in it is trusting men instead of God, and the Bible says that in doing so man is a fool.

7

MAN APPEARS ON EARTH

Even the atheistic evolutionists agree that man was the last creature to appear on earth. Man found everything ready for him to take over and to rule over. Did men appear before or after the Ice Age? Recent scientific theories seemingly have found evidence that man may be more than 3 million years old on earth. This theory is based on some footprints found around a volcano in Africa. But how can we tell that the footprint is really from man and not from an ape?

Some extravagant hypotheses try to explain the story of Paradise by sudden climate changes resulting from the Ice Age. This sudden cooling forced our ancestors to make tools and clothes to cover and protect themselves from the cold. It was pointed out by W. F. Albright in *From Stone Age to Christianity* that this theory is false. The cold climate of North America didn't produce any civilization. The Indians there adapted themselves to the cold but never developed a high culture, whereas the Incas and Mayas, in much more favorable circumstances, created a highly developed civilization.

All scientific theories that try to explain the early stages of human life on earth are based on the same spirit—atheism—as the theory of evolution. Their main purpose is to prove that the Bible is a collection of fairy tales and has nothing to do with facts, historical events. One of the main targets of this effort is the Fall of Man. Scientists try to prove that man never fell from a higher position; instead he was a savage beast and gradually evolved from beasthood into his present stage, a technical animal. But this stage is not yet final; it will lead to godhood. The road to godhood is knowledge, the famous apple of knowledge that Satan promised Eve would elevate us into godhood.

Let us consider an extreme case. Was Paradise on earth? If it was not, this would explain many things, particularly the major differences between man and the animals. The picture of Paradise in the Bible is so unreal, so out of this world, that one may suspect Paradise was somewhere else, not on this cursed earth. The scene described, where killer beasts lie in peace with animals that are supposed to be their prey in a blissful happiness unknown to us since that time, suggests that Paradise could not be here. Death and the food chain have always been part of life on earth, as ancient fossils tell us, as if this earth was created by Satan himself using God's power for his own purposes. Paradise, on the other hand, was pleasing to God, so much so that He Himself walked with Adam and Eve, teaching them many things. Earth somehow doesn't fit into this picture. Life on earth is a constant succession of birth and death, the food chain, which always has equated death for one with food for another.

Adam and Eve had to have different bodies from these we now have. Their bodies must have been capable of eternal life, since death entered our life only as the result of sin. As the result of disobedience to God, the blissful scene suddenly changed. Adam and Eve were expelled from Paradise. Life, which was an ever-changing wonder and amusement, suddenly became a hard task. They were cursed with labor, pain, and eventually death. The two scenes are so different that one may wonder if both were on the same planet.

Then consider this: Jesus said to the thief who was crucified with him, "Amen, I say to thee this day thou shalt be with me in paradise." Is this the same Paradise as that from which Adam and Eve were expelled? It may be, and this could explain many things. First of all, this clearly would indicate that Paradise is not in this three-dimensional world, since both Jesus and the thief would enter into it after the death of the body. The story of Adam and Eve seems to support this idea. They were not supposed to know death if they obeyed God. Death is part of the punishment for disobedience. Then they should have had a body capable of living eternally, something like the body Jesus had after His resurrection. As we know from the testimony of the apostles, Jesus was able to eat and to participate in life, but at the same time He was able to defy the laws of this material world. He was able to walk through closed doors, travel instantaneously, and, finally, go to Heaven without the help of a rocket. We can expect to have the same body as He had after our death, or the end of punishment at the end of the world. Did Adam and Eve have the same body in Paradise? I believe so, and when they were expelled this body was changed to flesh and blood as we now know it, which probably was created from the same material as the animal kingdom.

The whole process can even be explained using scientific language. As we saw, the substance of the atoms is energy. What we know as matter is only a particular form of this energy, not its only possible one. The laws governing the appearance of this energy can be changed. Such a change occurred at the resurrection of Christ. It is believed that the image of Christ on the burial cloth known to us as the Shroud of Turin is the result of radiation caused by such a change in the structure of the atoms. This radiation produced the three-dimensional image of Jesus Christ on the burial cloth.

Another riddle may be considered a further indication that Paradise was elsewhere and not on earth. The Bible tells us that two men were transported to Paradise without knowing death. One was the sixth descendent of Adam, Enoch, and the other was Elijah, who was taken by the fiery chariots of God. These two men are living in Paradise to this very day. As the fathers of the Church tell us, these two men are preserved till the days of Antichrist, and then they will be transported back to earth to testify against him. This is also a strong indication that Paradise still exists on another plane of reality, possibly in a higher dimension. Does this mean that the Garden of Eden was never on earth? That earth is only the place of punishment? No one can really answer this question.

Could this mean that Paradise was on some other planet of the universe, in another solar system? The thought is not impossible, as far as we know, since the universe exists in the fourth dimension, and we know nothing about life on other planets. Matter may exist in different forms on other planets of other solar systems or life exist in a form capable of eternal existence. But the possibility still exists that the human form of life was created first on earth, and God intended later to populate the universe, but because of His disappointment with men this plan was delayed until the end of the punishment and the winnowing of men. Jesus said, "I go to prepare a place for you," and He also assured us that there are many mansions in the house of Our Father.

Recently many clinically dead people who have been resuscitated have testified that life does not end but begins at the moment of death. Many were quite unhappy that they had to return into this animal prison that we know as our body after they had tasted new life on a higher dimension with unlimited possibilities. Unfortunately, organized religions neglect the subject and leave the interpretation to controversial spiritualist sects, which misuse and abuse it.

It is possible that, as part of the punishment, after the Fall, this animal body of ours was created with all its animal characteristics—instincts, limited abilities, exhaustion, pain, vulnerability, sickness, the pangs of birth, the unhappy process of aging, and, finally, death, the most feared of all.

This is one of the possibilities one may speculate on, but never can prove or disprove. It is the secret of God, not for us to know, at least not in this body. But if Paradise wasn't on earth, all the speculations of the atheists are false.

This possibility would not affect the reality of the Bible. As we have shown, it offers some indication that the location of Paradise was elsewhere. But even if it was on earth, Adam and Eve could still have had a body capable of eternal life, which could not be harmed by animals, including sickness-causing viruses and bacteria. In this form they were perfect, the real overlords of life on earth, able to enjoy it fully without any concern. Theirs was a state of perfect happiness that was lost after the original sin, when their body was transformed to the realm of animals, and the blissful scene of Paradise was lifted from earth.

But God didn't intend to leave man forever in that state. The punishment is for only a limited time, and those who pass this more difficult test can regain Paradise. God even promised this to Adam, and this is the most important inheritance we received from Him. God even promised a helper, a redeemer, who in the fullness of time will come and show us how to regain the original inheritance, Paradise. He sent His own Son, Jesus Christ, to become man, to take on Himself our sins, and to reconcile us with God, easing greatly our task of pleasing God. At least this is what we Christians believe.

Many don't understand the story of creation. One of the strangest things in it is the creation of Eve. But this could be considered as a very important message. It allows us to take a look at God's method and at the same time it can be conceived as proof that God always used one step to create the next, and did not create everything from inorganic matter. In this way a succession of creation can be envisioned, which, although it may resemble the philosophy of evolution, is light years away from it.

No man who accepts the existence of God can doubt the Fall of Man, unless he denies eternal life and all other truths of religion shared and handed down from Adam and Eve, who personally knew God and were the authors of this sad experience. Man had a much higher state of existence before the original sin, and as the direct consequence of his disobedience to God, man suddenly lost everything. Adam and Eve suddenly found themselves in a changed body with many limitations and disadvantages, and also in a changed environment, which no longer supplied them readily with all their needs but had to be persuaded by hard work to yield the bare necessities of life. Man not only wasn't accustomed to such a situation, but was even ill-equipped, compared with other animals, for the task. Imagine yourself, especially if you are a city dweller who knows vegetables only on the shelves and meat only in the icebox, suddenly finding yourself on a barren island or in uninhabited farmland, with your hands your only tool. You would have to invent everything, to force nature to feed you. So it was with our ancient parents. The carefree life of Paradise suddenly vanished, and trouble was everywhere. They never had heard how to cultivate the earth, how to sow, how to catch animals; their knowledge in Paradise was quite different from this.

Since they did not know anything at the start of their life on earth, at that stage one could say they were savages. But were they? Does the way you earn your bread determine your total ability, including intellectual ability? The answer must be no. Your total ability basically depends on your outlook on life, how you answer the most basic question in life: Why are we here on earth? The atheist who can't believe in God and eternal life will value this life above everything. Today even those who can accept the existence of God value this life more and more. Since they are not really sure about the other, they try to have a chance at both. Only those who believe in God without reservation can accept the fact that this earth is only a place of punishment, and that life on it is only a pilgrimage, that one has to collect not earthly but heavenly things, since no earthly thing can be carried with us. They know that life is only a test. It doesn't matter what you do in your individual life to earn your fare for the earthly journey; the only thing that matters is that you be careful not to fail the test, which is highly individualized and specialized. In that sense an abundance of material or intellectual wealth is a disadvantage. Both can easily divert attention from the real goal and can cause failure, with dreadful consequences.

While the original test was easy—at least so it seems to us— our tests are more complicated, as we are under punishment. The reward seems higher too, since if someone passes the test he will become the son of God, as promised by Jesus Christ, a position even higher than the status of the angels.

Many wonder about the origin of different religions. How did they come into existence if men are descended from only one ancestor? A complete new science has emerged from this, called the science of comparative religions. Some talk about the evolution of relgions; others say, not that God created man, but that man created God, by personifying common natural phenomena like lightning and thunder. I will surprise you now, because I believe that in a sense they are right. All the divine beings imagined throughout the ages are imperfect creations of men and do not resemble God at all, because God is beyond our imagination. We are unable to imagine the Creator of the Universe. For educational purposes, to communicate ideas about Him to the next generations, we have to make an imperfect sketch of the omnipotent God, but this doesn't mean that

He resembles this picture at all. When atheists attack these images they just reveal their immaturity, their inability to distinguish between reality and imagination.

Just imagine man at the beginning. After his painful Fall he must have been in a state of shock. Though men knew they deserved their punishment, they still would feel bitter and resentful toward God. God, on the other hand, was dissatisfied, too. This made relations between man and God rather chilly. As we saw, God rejected the offering of Cain, and this resulted in the first killing on earth. The first man who found favor with God was in the sixth generation after Adam. This man was Enoch, who walked with God, and whom God took from earth without letting him die. The Fathers of the Church tell us that Enoch, together with Elijah, live in Paradise, the same Paradise in which Adam and Eve lived, and see everything that happens on earth, and that they are wiser than all men together.

While the descendents of Adam, after Cain killed Abel, tried to please God, the descendents of Cain probably did not even try after the initial failure of their father. All of them became the fathers of tribes, later nations, and they carried on their own customs. Some tried to please God, but there was no written law saying how this should be done. No one was able to imagine God as He is; thus various cults started to flourish according to the individual ability of each nation, as we can reconstruct with greater or lesser accuracy from archeology. But probably our findings concern only the time after the flood, since the worldwide flood destroyed all artifacts that existed before.

By the time of the Great Flood, the wickedness of man was so great that God repented that He had created man (Genesis 6:5-6). The story of the Great Flood is one of the oldest religious inheritances of mankind. It can be found all over the world, in Asia, America, Australia, and so on, even among the myths of tribes that have had no contact with Western civilization. But watch out for the double standard of atheists. Though they can accept evolution without a single proof, there is no proof that would convince them that the Great Flood happened. Lyell's theory of uniformity was invented to disprove the possibility of the Flood.

The atheists of the last century were especially eager to disprove the Bible. They even were ready to go so far as to destroy evidence that seemed to prove the truth of the Bible. Such was the case with the Ark of Noah, which was found by European civilization around the turn of the century. The case of the three English "scientists" who found the Ark is well documented. They disguised themselves as religious persons to mislead the natives of Mount Ararat, and persuaded the natives to lead them to the Ark. When they saw that it was indeed the Ark described in the Bible, they became so angry that they tried to destroy it. Since this was impossible, they threatened to kill their native guides if they led others to the scene or even dared to talk about it. This is the highly praised impartiality and objectivity of science!

Velikovsky, on the basis of thousands of facts and pieces of evidence, clearly proved that the theory of uniformity is false. Cosmic catastrophes could have happened in the past, and could even have happened in the past few thousand years. One may reject his explanation of the wandering of the planet Venus, which supposedly caused the disturbances, but this doesn't exclude the possibility that some other huge meteorite came close enough to cause such a disturbance. God could have a thousand methods of interfering with life on earth. Recent changes in the orbit of the outer planet, Pluto, indicate the possibility that under some circumstances it is possible for a planet suddenly to change its orbit. Imagine what would happen if one of the outer satellites of the giant planets escaped from its present orbit and started wandering inside the solar system, causing disturbances in the orbits of the other planets. It could come too close to Earth, so close that Earth might be able to capture it as a second moon. Then just think, given the effect of the present moon on the earth's crust and the oceans, what effect a second moon might have.

Recently, there has been a compromise solution to the question of the Great Flood. Some scientists try to explain it as if it was only a local flood a bit out of proportion. But this would not explain why this flood is part of the myths of people so widely scattered all over the world. Some try to explain it as the melting of the ice after the Ice Age. But not even the Ice

Age has been proved beyond the shadow of a doubt. According to my interpretation, there was no ice age before this last one in the history of the earth as many suppose, even before life appeared. This was the first one, and it seems to have been asymmetrical. The forming of the ice started at the North Pole. Then it blocked the narrow sea passages, and since in doing so it blocked the paths of vital currents, thus it was possible to form a larger ice cap on the North Pole. The ice cap may have caused the wandering of the pole, perhaps in conjunction with some cosmic effect, as Velikovsky suspects. This asymmetry equalized later when ice formed on the South Pole, too. This does not suppose that a sudden melting resulting in a worldwide flood, but rather that a gradual cooling of the sea eventually made it possible for ice to form in the Antarctic, which is surrounded by sea.

Velikovsky proved that much evidence has been misinterpreted by science. Many phenomena attributed to the Ice Age can be explained better and more logically by the Flood. Among them are huge boulders transported to great distances, and fossils, remnants of animal matter and vegetation that can be found in caves in many places. These large graveyards contain tropical and cold-climate animals side by side, even beneath the thick cover of ice in the polar regions. Such finds can be explained only by a worldwide flood, supposing the animals to have been transported by water. Huge tidal waves starting in the tropics must have picked up animals there and headed toward the poles, picking up animals as they went and carrying them to a common burial ground, caves where they were preserved by the mud or ice.

Such a cosmic catastrophe must have caused tremendous changes on the surface of the earth. It certainly would have been able to destroy what man had created before the Flood. It may have included changes so drastic that dry land became permanently submerged and ocean floor became mountains. Velikovsky has doubts about just when the Alps or the Himalayas were formed. Geology places this event about 60 to 70 million years ago, but it may have happened a lot later, or have been finished during the Flood. Some legends of the ancient past talk about submerged continents like Atlantis or the Mu continent. Could such catastrophes be connected with the Great Flood? They may be, but science cannot or will not provide us with such information. Such changes can destroy civilizations without a trace. It is also conceivable that the population of the earth at that time was close to its present value, and there may have been very advanced knowledge and maybe even technology. The Ark itself is a wonder: even with modern technology one can't build a more stable vessel. But such a civilization can disappear without a trace. If our civilization were destroyed like that, what would remain of it ten thousand years from now? Not even concrete foundations.

History started a new chapter after the Flood. Even if we suppose that Noah and his family possessed all the knowledge of their time, which is unlikely, they could not preserve it under their changed circumstances. The emphasis again was on the provision of bare necessities, and though I imagine they would have tried to teach their offspring the things they remembered, much of their knowledge would no longer make sense, since no such things could be seen around them any more. After a few generations, all knowledge would have faded away, except some remnants surviving as legends of the past. Some were even modified beyond recognition. Later this knowledge was preserved only by a few priests as tiny scraps of the original knowledge.

Just think, how much knowledge could survive our age if this civilization were destroyed, and only an average family like Noah's survived? In such circumstances, how much physics, or technical know-how, or medicine would survive? Only some legends about fiery machines that flew in the sky, or carriages that went by themselves would remain.

The basic fundamentals, however, had survived with Noah and his family. Among these was the most basic: religion. The essence of all religion is the recognition of an omnipotent God above us and a set of rules telling us how to please this God, who has a lot to do with our fate. The methods of pleasing God differ in various parts of the world, but the essence is the same everywhere. All religions try to establish some standard of what is pleasing and what is displeasing to God in people's life-styles. Before the Great Flood it was thought that burning sacrifices was the most pleasing to God. Thus Noah burned sacrifices after the Flood, too, and this method of pleasing God spread as his descendents scattered over the new surface of the earth. Abraham pleased God in the same way, and the sacrifice of animals is the essence of the Mosaic religion, too. Religions can differ in customs; in some places the original monotheism may have degenerated into polytheism, depending on how people perceived what God wants from them. All religion is colored by the individual soul of the race. If we accept—as we should—the existence of Satan, then we can assume that he influenced people, too, bending them to worship him or simply confusing their ideas.

Christianity gave a new, universal meaning to the relation between God and man. In Jesus Christ, God fulfilled His promise to Adam of a redeemer, who would straighten out the relationship strained by the original sin. Christ's single blood sacrifice made the old ritual meaningless and put the relation on a higher level.

If man is not an individual creation, but gradually developed from the ape, then in our time we would witness monkeys at different levels of evolution, the transition between man and the apes. Many such steps would have to exist side by side. No such thing has ever been observed. I didn't elaborate in this chapter why in the past man wasn't a savage, but many others have done so. I believe the question is simply ridiculous, and not worth serious consideration. Besides, it is a vanity when the individual elevates himself above his brute ancestors. A person who has never asserted this must consider that without the ingenuity of his ancestors he would never have reached the extent of his present knowledge.

Man was never a savage beast. Our modern civilization produces more savages than ever existed on the face of the earth. The first man may not have known how to build or how to cultivate the land, but this doesn't mean he was a savage. His previous higher state didn't provide such knowledge, but he knew a lot more about God, a subject grossly neglected today. Though modern man knows many things about his surroundings and how to use them for his own good, to make life easier and, by that, in a sense to cheat the curse of God, this knowledge may prove to be counterproductive, to be degradation and not progress. Man has lost sight of the horizon, his goal on earth, to know and serve God, and has exchanged his bright future for some shortlived comforts, chasing earthly happiness—never to be found—and losing eternal joy and eternal life.

8

IS HISTORY AN EXACT SCIENCE?

If you take a look at your youngster's history book, you will learn, if you do not yet know, that man in the early ages was a savage animal. This animal slowly learned to use tools, first crude stones and sticks, then combinations of the two. The male of the species hunted for animals, while the female gathered seeds and other vegetables. If you saw some pictures illustrating the early ages of mankind, you probably will never forget the scene of the brutal male carrying a big stick in one hand while with the other he pulls after him the female, his mate, by the hair. Did you ever see an example of such "love" in the animal kingdom? It was designed to prove what a brutal being man was, to contradict the biblical account of the Fall of man. Numerous films present this view, as do television and other mass-communication media, to illustrate ineradicably in the minds of your children the misconception that man never had a higher status, as the Bible says, but instead was a brutal, savage animal. I do not want to believe that my ancestors were like this. Do you?

Most people think the teachers must know what they teach, and that certainly scientists are fair enough not to want to fool the world. They think that if the teachers and the scientists make such a claim, they must have plenty of evidence, and there is thus no choice but to accept the unpleasant truth about our ancestry. But they have no evidence. Just as in the case of evolution, the missing links are still missing. However, we have more evidence here than is the case with evolution. We have a few crude rock tools that may have been used by the first men. But, as I showed in Chapter 7, Adam and Eve had to start somewhere after they suddenly found themselves in a hostile environment. The most ancient relics of mankind show that even man was the same as he is now. These relics show that man was intelligent and that he appeared suddenly on earth. Although he used crude tools, this doesn't mean he was behind us intellectually. Just the opposite of this may prove to be true, that he in many ways was superior to today's atheists.

But don't expect atheists to admit that. They never compromise. They think that if they repeat a lie often enough it will become truth. For example, Carl Sagan announced on his television show "Cosmos"—in an uplifted, exalted manner, like a religious truth—that evolution is no longer a theory, it is a fact, while lifting up his eyes as the priest in the Mass does when he carries out the transubstantiation. No, it is not a fact but a lie, and it is a lie not by chance (the new god), but by purposeful deception. It is a dogma of atheism, in our days regarded as sacrosanct.

There is no missing link to prove that man slowly evolved from monkeys. No, all evidence suggests that man suddenly appeared on earth with his full intelligence, but with primitive technology. The few artifacts that we have from that age, such as cave paintings and a few stone tools, can be interpreted as one may wish, to fit into any and even opposing views on history. But they will never support the atheists' claim about the savagery of our ancestors. Yes, God may have taken the matter of the earth and developed it slowly into the monkey, but from that same matter He instantaneously created man as He imagined him in the first place, the crown of creation. The Bible never made a secret of the fact that our body is one with the matter of the earth, neither does it say that it was created in some manner as a sculpture is worked from clay, but it clearly states that man is the last piece of creation, the crown of it, and that he is set apart from the animal kingdom.

As an example of just how misleading our interpretation of the past can be, let us consider the following imaginary case. Archeologists, the fact-finders of history, discover a rather large barrel or tub with a few necessities of life in it, indicating that it was someone's dwelling place. Using the basic technique of comparing the findings with recent examples, the archeologists conclude that the fellow who used this barrel as his apartment must have been an ancient bum, a being of low intelligence, who failed to find his place in life and relapsed to the level of animal existence. The truth might be in sharp contrast to this. This man might have been the most brilliant man of his age, the philosopher Diogenes (412-323 B.C.). Of course, this is an exaggerated example, but just imagine how many of such misinterpretations may have burdened our knowledge of the past.

Isn't it obvious that atheists want to see brutal animals in the past in order to prove their thesis that man never fell but slowly evolved to his present peak of knowledge, knowledge that may prove to be fatal to the destiny of mankind?

Our ancestors didn't have the high technology that we have; not even our grandfathers had it, and does this mean that they were less men than we are? Isn't just the opposite of this true? Our vast and dubious knowledge more and more brings forth the animal in us. For examples of this, one just has to watch the local news on television. A mighty, proud, and basically foreign philosophy is gaining ground in our days, saying that everything in the past is inferior, ignorant, and savage, while we are the superior species of our race. There must be something wrong with this philosophy. It is like digging out the roots of a tree and wondering why it will die soon.

Even the earliest evidence about the life of mankind on earth suggests that men were intelligent beings, lived in communities, and helped and loved each other while they struggled with the cursed earth to take from it their livelihood. They believed in God, and in life after death.

Many historians admit that history is not an exact science. Just how one may interpret history depends on one's philosophical background. An individual saturated with atheistic philosophy will try to fit the few artifacts that we have from the past into his individual, godless perception of the world. But unfortunately the opposite of this is no longer true, because historians with a religious background no longer dare to express dissenting opinions, since atheism is the ruling philosophy in scientific life. Only materialistic, atheistic views are taken seriously in science, and any dissent is silenced and condemned as unscientific as soon as it surfaces. The best example of this is the case of Velikovsky, who was immediately condemned and ridiculed, not only by his colleagues, who, if they had dared to be impartial, would have had to admit that his ideas are one plausible explanation of many unsolved problems, but also in completely unrelated areas, like the attack by Rudolf Flesch in a book on English style. This author, who knows nothing about the subject, casually mentioned in his book that scientists enjoyed a hearty laugh at Velikovsky's ideas. Why such a broad attack against a man who dared to step out of cliches? Because he dared to say that the stories of the Bible may actually have happened, and that miracles can have a natural explanation. He dared to doubt the second dogma of atheism, evolution, and dared to think originally about man's past. He left the door open for compromise with atheism, but even this didn't help him. There is no compromise possible between religion and atheism. Why? Because both are religions, but with different gods. One of them must be falsely claiming godhood, because both can't be true.

Today the views of atheism prevail in all walks of life. The dogmas of this new religion are just as sacrosanct and partial as the views of religion were in earlier ages. While religious education is forbidden in schools, the views of atheism are vigorously taught everywhere, in the name of secularism and impartiality. Since students hear only one voice, opposing the idea of religion, we should not wonder why our youth turn out to be atheists when they finish their education. How could they decide about the truth when they hear only one side of the question? Education all over the world produces atheists in a wholesale fashion, who ridicule the real truth of religion, since they have been taught that it is ridiculous.

This is true in all sciences, but certainly most true in the case of history. Many reputable historians ask the question: Is impartiality possible in reconstructing history? Since there are a limited number of artifacts and they could fit into many, even opposing, interpretations, many have come to the conclusion that no real knowledge of history is possible. History in many cases becomes only a tool for propaganda. This is obvious behind the Iron Curtain, where the communist government openly confesses atheism as the state religion. There everything serves to spread this official view, and it is quite natural that atheist propaganda prevails in the explanation of history, as in any other science, and in mass-communications media. But it is hard to understand why the same propaganda prevails in education here in the free, so-called Christian West. Behind the Iron Curtain all relics of the past must fit into shallow, propagandistic explanations. What does not fit is made to fit, and unfortunately the same method is used here.

Historians complain that there is no key to unlock the secrets of the past. But they blindly pass by the only valid key: God. God is the only one who can shed light on past events and on the future, as well. Religion is the only philosophy that can explain history, a philosophy written in the Bible, but a philosophy no longer considered valid. Without this key, written in the Bible, history is a chaos of unrelated events, a meaningless struggle, a cosmic drama without any happy ending in sight. The Bible preserves all the history of mankind necessary to understand why we are here and what the struggle is all about, even if it sometimes seems to us that only one page has remained from a thick book, and that is the table of contents. With God, history is a simple, understandable process, with a definite start and a certain end. It is the story of mankind's pilgrimage on earth, a place of punishment, which will end in time and be followed by an eternal existence on a higher dimension. This explanation is the most ancient inheritance of mankind, originating from the first man who set foot on this cursed earth. Earth is a penal colony, not the site of a pleasure trip. The first men, Adam and Eve, knew God personally. They passed this knoweldge on to their children. It no longer was direct, personal knowledge, but it preserved an image of God and of how men should relate to Him. This is the most basic of all knowledge, the most ancient wisdom of mankind.

As I stated before, we know nothing of the time before the Great Flood. The Flood destroyed everything. History started a new chapter after this terrible catastrophe, the fearful wrath of God. We have no positive date as to just when this flood occurred. For me the most reliable calculation seems the computation of the negative growth rate. A friend of mine, a computer engineer, put into a powerful computer the data of the present population of earth and the average growth rate and ordered the computer to go back in time to the point when only one family existed. By using different values for the growth rate, the computer placed the time of Noah between 6 and 10 thousand years. We know, however, that our traceable history dates back only 5 thousand years. *The oldest civilization,* interestingly enough, *can be found on the foothills of Mount Ararat,* the landing place of the Ark of Noah in Mesopotamia, around the Tigris and Euphrates rivers. But this doesn't prove to the blind atheists the truth of the Bible. The very old culture of Egypt is only the daughter of this, together with the cultures of India and China. Recent archeological findings seem to suggest that people from these ancient Middle Eastern cultures reached the shores of America by ships. It is possible that the higher cultures of the Incas and Mayas also originated from that region; thus two different migrations may have populated America.

Velikovsky has proved that the recent climate of the earth is the result of polar changes about 3,800 years ago, around the time of Moses. Before that period the present inhospitable polar regions were inhabited by animals like the mammoth and many other temperate-climate animals. Thus the descendents of Noah were able to migrate by land to America. The nice climate in Siberia was a tempting hunting and fishing ground, and the Bering Strait didn't pose any obstacle to this migration. The present dating of this migration is based on the theory of a land bridge over the Bering Strait. It could be wrong. The fact that the Indians of America know about the Great Flood proves —to me at least—that the story of the Bible is true, and that the Indians are descendents of Noah, just as we are.

Many doubt the story of the Flood because of the diversity of language, customs, and religious beliefs in different parts of the earth. But this diversity is quite natural, even if Noah and his family had the same language and customs. There are living examples of how language can change during a few short centuries. Such an example can be seen in Central Europe, where German settlers formed isolated language islands within nations speaking different languages. In those islands, the language did not develop or, if it did, it developed in a different direction from that in Germany. After World War II, when these people were forced to go back to their native land, they barely understood the language. A less obvious example is the different dialects that exist in large countries, despite interconnections, especially in our age of mass communication.

Even if Noah and his family spoke a highly developed language, after the Flood only the most necessary words would have survived when life once again became primitive. The reduced vocabulary then could have drastic changes as people were separated by time and distance. A similar fate awaited their customs and their religion. This was the time of repopulating the earth. One may wonder what the religion of Noah could have been. It must have been monotheistic, and probably we are not far from the truth if we suppose it was similar to Abraham's religion. As we know, most ancient religions consider the burning of sacrifices to be their main act. Actually, every religion is only a set of customs by which an individual or a group tries to gain the favor of God. As people got separated, this set of customs could have changed radically, although retaining the main act, the burning of sacrifices. This process can be seen as a slow drift away from the original religion or, as one historian put it, as the degradation of monotheism into polytheism. But one may never be quite sure, even if one encounters a seemingly polytheistic culture, that in reality it is indeed polytheistic. If such a religion has a central God who is above the pantheon of supernatural beings, then it may be considered basically monotheistic, though decorated with new ideas. Such a development depends on the individual spirit of a particular race or tribe.

We know how strong a mark an individual can place on the religion of a region. Just think about Buddha, or Zoroaster, or Moses. But none of them claimed to be a god, to be the Son of God, the promised Messiah. Buddha even predicted Jesus in the Diamond Sutra. He said that a man would come five hundred years after his death who would be as great as ten thousand Buddhas, and called on his followers to harken to him.

One of the main arguments against the originality of the Bible is that the events described in it can be found elsewhere in the secret books of other religions of the region. This proves —some say—that the Bible is just another set of ancent myths and legends of the Middle East. But since when did such similarities prove that the Bible is not the authentic message of God? The Bible, in a sense, contains the whole history of mankind, and later the history of the Jewish nation. But the history of mankind was commonly known at that time in that region; thus it must have been part of all books that tried to give a complete account of mankind. The differences between accounts must derive from the fact that this history of mankind was kept for a long time as an oral tradition; thus it was subject to degradation. This is why we have only the table of contents, not the detailed history of mankind. Moreover, I believe that stories were exchanged at that time, since storytelling was the only intellectual entertainment, and so these ancient stories would have become widely known.

One of the critical stories mentioned as proof by atheists is the story of Joseph. It was found written in Egypt, but the names were changed, and this story was known to many other nations as their own. The question is: Did the Jews adopt the story because of its pious teaching, or did others find it so beautiful that they adopted it as their own? I believe it was first part of the Jewish heritage. Two things seem to support this belief. First, it is a clear explanation of how the Jews got to Egypt, where they later were enslaved. Second, I believe the symbolic meaning of the story represents the relation between the Jews and Jesus.

There is nothing peculiar about the attacks of the atheists on fundamental religious truths, such as the Bible. It is quite natural for them to try to discredit the foundation of our faith. The problems start, however, when priests start to believe in their attractive lies. Such is the case with the supposedly scientific "Higher Criticism." There is a peculiar thing about faith, namely, that it starts where reason stops. Thus to approach faith through reason may mean the loss of faith. For example, reason can never understand the divine nature of Jesus Christ. To a rationalist, Jesus was only a poor rabbi, a good man, who happened to be in the wrong place at the wrong time, which led to his early death. Since His teaching was well received in that particular part of the world and His disciples were enthusiastic zealots, Christianity spread like brushfire. A rationalist never could understand the divine care of the Holy Spirit in the spreading of Christianity. Without that supernatural care, Christianity still would be nothing, if it existed at all, other than a small Jewish sect. One needs to have the particular state of mind called grace to grasp higher reality, higher dimensions.

Atheists first took the Old Testament apart into small pieces. They compared the historical descriptions in it with their own archeological findings and declared that historical events are recorded inaccurately in the Bible. But who can be the judge of this? Apparently their judgment of the reconstruction of the history of the region was polluted by their atheistic explanations. There is a clear tendency in such criticism, and this tendency is: anything is better than the Bible. Every written document found elsewhere is immediately declared superior to or more authentic than our Holy Book. It is just as if, in a later age, when our civilization was being excavated, archeologists declared the writings of the Jehovah's Witnesses superior to other Christian documents. The Bible preserved quite naturally the common inheritance of mankind, but it did more. In it was preserved the most important message, the promise to Adam of the redeemer, the Messiah, who would relieve mankind of its burden of punishment. This message was forgotten by others, and Abraham was probably chosen to preserve it, along with other points of view. Why should we believe that any other record of the common inheritance of mankind is more accurate than the Bible?

The Bible is also the history of the Jewish people. This history was written to show the Jews how God cared about them, how He directed the slowly unfolding human drama throughout history. The recording of historical events is not necessarily the same in two neighboring countries. For example, if in a war one subdues the other, it certainly will be preserved in the records of the victor, but it may be minimized or eradicated in the records of the victim. On the other hand, the history of the region does not necessarily affect all nations in that area. Thus no one should expect a correct record of Middle Eastern history from the Bible, as we may reconstruct it today from our distance in time.

The attack on the historicity of the Bible was, however, a low-key issue. The fiercest attacks were focused on the prophets and the prophecies. Applying different tactics, the atheists want us to believe that the prophets never existed, that they are only fictional persons, part of a deliberate forgery by priests with the pious intent of giving psychological strength to the people at troubled times in their history. They say the prophecies are nothing but a particular style of writing, a backward-forward method, and that they were written hundreds of years after they are dated, long after the events described had taken place. Prophecies had nothing to do with the future, not even then, and certainly not now.

It troubles me to recall such a lie here, but one may get used to it if it appears in an atheist publication. But printed in a widespread religious magazine, it must be considered a crime—a crime greater than murder because it kills countless souls. It is contrary to the most basic articles of our faith, condensed in the apostolic creed, clearly stating that we believe God directed His people through the prophets. There is no doubt that this is a malicious lie, especially in our age, when we are witnessing the fulfillment of those ancient prophecies. From Moses to Jesus, each prophet predicted the universal dispersion of the Jewish people and their miraculous gathering before the end of time from all nations in the rebirth of Israel. Those prophets also describe the nuclear war against the newly gathered Israelites. The present clear fulfillment of these ancient promises is the best refutation of all those lies. This clearly proves that the prophets were real and that they spoke the word of God.

Of course, the real purpose of the attempts to discredit the Bible is to discredit Jesus. If the prophecies were false, then Jesus's claim to be the true Messiah cannot be valid either, since it was based, to a large extent, on these prophecies. This way Jesus can be considered only as a good man with a wrong attitude toward the rulers of His time, since atheists do not yet dare to call Him a common criminal.

After the attacks on the Old Testament, the atheists focused their attention on the New Testament. Using the old method, they took to pieces the four gospels, and piece by piece declared them forgeries, actualized legends of the past applied to the life of Jesus in order to make Him more popular. Miracles were dismissed as nonsense, invented after the fact in the natural process of a legend's growth. The same fate awaited the letters of the apostles. They proved to be, in atheists' eyes, also forgeries. Then came under scrutiny the early writings of the Church Fathers, which were declared to be stupid superstitions, almost at the level of black magic. They called all this mud-slinging science, not only science, but "Higher Criticism." Unfortunately, their ideas gained ground in the official stand of many Christian denominations, especially in theological schools, and finally the dirty flood reached the last stronghold of Christianity, the Catholic Church.

There is an interesting episode in this mud-slinging contest. During the last century, atheists ridiculed the concept of the protecting crystal spheres around the earth, declaring it most unscientific. However, this concept proved to be true, even if it needed to be modified a little. In the 1950's the spheres were discovered. We call them the Van Allen belts. It turned out that without these protective shields life would not be possible on earth because of intensive ultraviolet rays and cosmic rays carrying deadly high-energy particles. Thus it turned out that our ancestors were not that stupid after all. How many such discoveries still await us?

The sort of "rationalization of the faith" expressed in the "Higher Criticisms" is the only real reason behind the falsification of history. It serves only one purpose: to discredit Jesus Christ by discrediting the Bible. This very carefully orchestrated attack has deceived many. But who is the coordinator of such attacks? The answer is easy for those who accept the truth of the Bible. It is the archenemy of God and mankind: Satan. Trouble came to mankind through him, and trouble has been brewed by him throughout history. Satan commands formidable forces with the intent of sweeping mankind away from God. He is superior to man. Without God's active help and protection, man is only a toy in Satan's hand. Satan, with his many deceiving lies dressed out in alluring fashion, is certainly a major factor in history. Many peculiarities of history are the direct result of his intervention. Atheists reject the existence of God and by that reject His protection, knowingly or unknowingly choosing Satan instead of God. They become his slaves, and through them Satan carries out his plans. He suggests ideas to them, and these ideas may appear to be truth, since he is the master mixer, mixing truth with lies and putting the rest in an attractive, logical form, just as we see in the case of evolution. He certainly is the main patron of reconstructing history to prove the validity of atheism.

There is a growing tendency in our evaluation of the past, a proud tendency basically foreign to the traditional thinking of mankind. We tend to see every past event and all past life as inferior to ours. We are the great, the unbeatable, the champions of life. Mankind is thought to have had a childhood and later an adolescence, and we are thought to have reached adulthood. But not everybody agrees with such an evaluation. T.S. Eliot, for example, wrote that we have traded wisdom for knowledge, and knowledge for information. Thus we are better informed about many things, basically about our surroundings, but might this not mean that we are less wise?

9

THE DUBIOUS BLESSINGS OF PROGRESS

We are very proud of our new gadgets—new toys produced by technology, like the car, the many electrical gadgets, airplanes, and rockets that are even able to carry us to the moon. As far as we know, no previous generation on earth ever had such toys, and there is no end of this marvelous progress in sight. If we chart time and progress we get a slowly rising curve, which suddenly accelerates upward almost vertically in a short period of time. The comparison with previous times is amazing. There was almost no progress at all during the traceable five-thousand-year history of mankind compared with our time, when progress got off the ground about a hundred years ago and since then has been increasing with astonishing speed.

What made this incredible progress possible?

The main reason is a radical change in how we perceive reality, a 180° shift in the direction of thinking. In previous ages there was a great resistance to any change, any progress. This seems almost built into the subconscious of those times, as if they knew that the age of technology had not yet arrived. This attitude wasn't the invention of the Middle Ages, or the widely accused Catholic Church. Legend says that a glassmaker in the Roman Empire invented a way to mass-produce glass. The local provincial governor was so impressed with the invention that he presented the glassmaker to Caesar, hoping to get some reward. Caesar ordered the execution of the inventor. When the astonished governor asked why, Caesar said, "Can you imagine how many other glassmakers would become unemployed if we let this man succeed?" And he continued, "Do you know what this could mean? It could mean rebellion and eventually the collapse of the Empire." He was right. The seemingly innocent inventions that started to flourish in the seventeenth century brought about the total collapse of the feudal system. Does this mean that those feudal rulers weren't wise enough to recognize the threat, or simply that the time finally had arrived for the age of technology? I believe the last is true, and that this is not the product of chance, but an effective interference by supernatural forces, which I believe are carefully monitoring and directing life on earth. I further believe that each new step of progress is inspired by them.

Progress started around the sixteenth century with the basic discoveries of science. The roadblock against it, the universal Church, after a thousand-year period of quiet was successfully removed by being split into pieces, which were directed against each other. Technology played an important role in bringing about this division. Without the novelty of printing, invented just in time, the split could not have been so successful, or even possible. The ruling philosophy that "blocked progress" for a thousand years in the "dark ages" was drastically changed during a short period of time. Previous ages embraced a philosophy that rejected or completely neglected life on earth. They focused their attention on the promised eternal life after death. Of course it would be naive to think that everybody shared this view, but during this period it was the ruling philosophy. In this point of view, earth was only a valley of tears, through which one must make a pilgrimage to reach perfection and to secure a good place in the afterworld, where real life began. Those people wanted only the bare essentials from earth, and if life was short, that was for the best, since that way eternal happiness would start earlier. Their eyes were focused on heaven, not on earth. This attitude changed drastically when Christianity was split. The worldly spirits who initiated the split doubted or straightforwardly rejected the philosophy of the previous age. They gained the upper hand in both religious and secular life. Since they were not sure about the afterlife or rejected it altogether, they naturally wanted to take advantage of this life, perhaps the only one they would have, and they tried to get the most out of it they could. They rejected the merit of suffering, so highly praised in previous ages. They didn't want to suffer at all. They wanted to enjoy life instead. The love of neighbor was exchanged for the love of profit. The way to profit was to exploit others, and the classic phase of capitalism had begun. This new method, or economic order, created suffering, poverty, and misery for many in order to provide luxury for a few. However, we don't have to go to Marx to learn something of this age; we have only to read Dickens or Victor Hugo to get a grasp of how this new stage of progress worked.

The Industrial Revolution, it seemed, could solve many of the problems of the previous stage of progress. But the workers didn't perceive it this way. They saw only that machines had taken away the few and miserable jobs they had, and in their blind anger they rebelled against this progress. In many places they broke the machines. Actually this process has not yet ended. Wise machines take away men's jobs even today, but we no longer break those machines. They show up only as a statistic, the growing number of surplus people, the unemployed.

If we dig into the essence of this marvelous technology, it turns out that basically it is very simple. In most cases it is nothing but an imitation of how men work. Just think about construction machines, shovels, and diggers. The same principle applies in factories too; in a slightly more complicated, more organized fashion, machines there also imitate men at work. Taking away the hardship and boredom of monotonous work should be seen as an asset, if everybody benefits from it. But this isn't the case most of the time. Many people are excluded from the benefits, while others take more than their share. This leads to conflict, violating the principle of equality, not to mention the law of love.

Our technology is based on an unlimited supply of energy. But, as it is turning out, our energy supply is anything but unlimited. To generate energy we still use the ancient method, fire, which was known to the first men on earth. As we saw, this method requires the rearrangement of chemical bonds to a more stable form. Mostly we burn oil to generate heat, which we in an inefficient way turn into other forms of energy. If the oil supply is depleted in the near future, the whole structure of our society will collapse. The discovery of nuclear fission raised hope. It was a major step toward assuring a continuous energy supply. But even with this we are tapping a limited supply of energy. Nuclear fusion would provide us with the ultimate, perhaps unlimited, supply of energy, but despite high hopes that have been raised from time to time, this sort of energy generation is still far from economically feasible if it is possible at all. Our world of technology resembles a balloon that was quickly inflated with lots of energy. If we are not careful enough, it can rupture at any time. Technology is the by-product of an effort to create more and more effective tools for war, to enable soldiers to kill more and more persons in a shorter period of time and from greater distances. Machines or gadgets were later modified in the pauses between wars to serve our convenience. As we gather more and more gadgets around us, we believe we free ourselves from hard work, and have more time for pleasure, called recreation, but this is simply an illusion. Today we are busier than ever. Not only the man of the family has to go to work, but even the woman does, thus leaving the children to be raised on the streets, or by television. In a sense, not only do gadgets not serve us, but we are slowly becoming *their* slaves. Many sociologists and artists have recognized that technology, by creating artificial surroundings for us, actually has cut the tie between man and nature. The newly created artificial atmosphere has resulted in alienation, frustration, loneliness, and many other abnormal, pathological symptoms or, in a word, in the crisis of the soul.

The big steps of progress achieved during the past few centuries are heralded today as great, but if we scratch the surface of this great progress, many steps today seem not only not wise but even an unwarranted, careless interference in the wise ways of nature. For example, atheists accuse the Church of blocking the progress of medicine in the Middle Ages. Hospitals to care for the sick were Christian inventions, but they avoided interfering with the way nature regulated the number of people living on the earth. From the perspective of time, it seems that the Church was right when it opposed major interference with nature's way—when, for example, it opposed the institution of vaccination as a preventive measure. The rapid development of medicine resulted in the greatest menace of our time: the population explosion. If we had let nature take care of the population problem, we wouldn't have known overpopulation for a long time. Some scientists see this problem as more threatening than nuclear war in our time. Today we save every lame, cripple with superior technology, while we kill billions and billions of healthy individuals before they are born, and yet we still have the Damoclean sword of overpopulation above our heads.

There must be a limit to just how many people the earth can support. By the year 2000 it is estimated that the population of the earth will grow by 50 percent—the present 4 billion people will be 6 billion. No such crowd can be provided even with the bare necessities, and we know everybody wants more than that. Thus the problem, even in a rigidly organized world society, seems unsolvable, especially if we consider that the growth is concentrated in underdeveloped countries, where even today it creates crises. All this is the direct result of our careless interference with nature's ways.

The greatest impact technological development had was on agriculture. The small farms gradually were eliminated and replaced by huge agricultural industries. People were also replaced by machinery, and lately by chemicals. The new methods and the application of chemicals promised an increased yield of agricultural products. This was especially promising in the already overpopulated areas of the world, the Third World countries. The high hopes, however, soon faded away. The new techniques require lots of energy, energy that is in short supply in most of those countries, not to mention water, which also is becoming scarce. The whole new progress in agriculture has turned out to be only wishful thinking in most parts of the world. There are no agricultural miracles possible. New lands can't be brought into production unless we irreparably damage the environment.

The new agricultural methods require that fewer and fewer people be employed in agriculture. This has resulted in a continuous and ever-increasing current of people moving from rural areas to the major cities. In our days this uprooted crowd swells the cities to an incredible size. These people don't find their place in the cities, becoming a hopeless, alienated proletariat, a new form of slaves, susceptible to new atheistic ideas and to communism. The slums of the big cities are anything but a healthy environment for the soul. The abnormal swelling of the cities has created countless new problems and countless new forms of suffering. The problems of the cities are well known, since they are the subject of every newscast. People living together require laws to regulate this association. If a larger number of people live together, the importance of these laws becomes more visible. They must be accepted by all and enforced with the utmost rigor. Such should be the case in the big cities. But this isn't so. Instead, society has adopted a philosophy contrary to this: permissiveness has become the name of the game. The result of this new permissive society is before us: chaos, lawlessness, and all kinds of flourishing sin—an environment hostile to morality and to God. The mass media, especially television, have become the apostles of this permissiveness, praising criminals, making heroes of them, while ridiculing decency and moral, law-abiding people. Television has become a tool for brainwashing, influencing society in a previously unprecedented way, making it hostile to traditional values and promoting mostly atheistic ideas.

One of the newest creations of progress is the chemical industry. Chemistry has produced previously unknown associations of atoms—chemicals—on an astonishing scale with great speed. Most of the new chemicals are poisons. The application of these chemicals has created a situation unimaginable before, the large-scale pollution of the environment. This in the long run even threatens to eliminate mankind from the earth. Chemicals are the cause of many new illnesses, such as the increase in cancer. Our new lifestyle, especially in the cities, creates an ocean of polluted water. Our rivers turn into sewers, sewers that pour their contents into the oceans, polluting and eventually killing life in them. As Cousteau stated, if the oceans die, we won't survive them, either. And all of this is happening in the name of progress.

One of the most sophisticated new gadgets we have is the computer. It is admittedly a marvelous tool, and helps us in many ways. But the wide application of computers has created a set of myths about them, especially in the realm of science fiction. In some fantastic stories the computer has become an almost omnipotent being. In reality, however, if we combined all the computers of the world, they still wouldn't be able to match the average brain. Even if computers become more sophisticated in the future, they will remain only tools.

One of the most prominent applications of computers is space research. But space research, too, is only the by-product of military technology, only a demonstration for our opponents, of our capability. It is a tool of psychological warfare. The main feature of our technology is the development of weapons, a highly efficient form of destruction, capable of destroying civilization on earth. The claim, though, that we are capable of destroying the earth itself is invalid. We don't have such power and probably never will.

Technology, the most visible result of progress, is basically destructive in nature. Through countless miseries it cuts man off from nature and puts more and more effective weapons into the hands of dictators, sometimes insane ones, with which to exterminate the people of the earth. Thanks to technological development, the number of victims increased tenfold from World War I to World War II, and today we are capable of eliminating half of mankind in mere hours.

Knowledge is increasing so rapidly that it has created a flood of information, which we have difficulty even storing. The number of people who have access to vital information is getting smaller (and the possibility of invasion of privacy is increasing). The gap between informed and uninformed people is widening. Access to information has created a new elite, which possesses and uses it for its own advantage, while more and more people are becoming underinformed, which eventually shows up as economic disadvantage. In our streets, particularly in the big cities, people representing the two opposite ends of the scale exist side by side. Lots of people possess so little knowledge that they are not much above the level of primitive men of the jungle, possessing only a predatory instinct. On the other hand, a small number of people are on or even above the increased level of knowledge of the twentieth century.

An example of this contradiction, which is becoming a conflict, is the case of the world-renowned German economics professor who was killed in the streets of New York. The professor, invited to be a guest lecturer at Columbia University, decided to take a walk after the lecture, as he used to do in his native land. A gang of youths surrounded him and demanded his gold wristwatch. He resisted, and his brilliant brain was poured out on the pavement. The attackers escaped with the watch, never to be found. Maybe ten similar brains exist, but there are countless such predatory youths, below the level of animals.

This sad situation exists despite the fact that knowledge is offered on a silver plate for everybody free. Never in history has a society done as much. Everybody can get free education through 12 consecutive years until maturity, and yet the majority of the youth reject this unheard-of opportunity. They don't want to possess knowledge. The free high school system is becoming a baby-sitting service for adolescent youth. About 10 percent would like to learn, but the rest of the gang blocks their sincere efforts. In our days we are witnessing the total failure of the educational system, despite the fact that we spend more and more on education. Schools are becoming the hunting grounds of young criminals, who attack students and teachers alike. Illiterate youths are given diplomas just to get rid of them as soon as possible. The school system is not differentiated, as in other parts of the world, where students can choose between schools that prepare them appropriately for life, and competition is completely eliminated, in sharp contrast to life, where competition is severe. Requirements are dropped year by year in order to save students from boredom. Isn't that the total failure of science, too?

Learning and knowledge have always been a privilege, and they still are in most parts of the world. Students, however, must have a goal, a reason why they have to study, a painfully hard enterprise requiring dedication. But no such thing is visible in the American school system. In other parts of the world, strict discipline is required from students. Undisciplined youth are thrown out of the schools, together with underachievers; thus school crime is unknown in other parts of the world. Without education, only the lowest-paying jobs are available; thus students know that it is worthwhile to study. They know that the higher achievers are getting higher-paying jobs.

In the Soviet Union, the counterpart of our society, scientists are the highest-esteemed citizens. A university degree means a privileged place in society. Scientists are protected, so much so that there are even separate cities for scientists. Not only do we not protect scientists, but many times they are thrown out of jobs and forced to stand in unemployment lines like the most common stock of mankind. Not to mention the other highly educated people—the engineers, or teachers, or chemists and physicists. These people are regarded as highly skilled workers, but that does not exempt them from job insecurity and concern for the future. Since learned men are not regarded as special, why should we wonder that youths see no reason why they should go through the painful process of learning? This society rewards merchants: a businessman with a mediocre mind and a limited number of special skills can make more money than a university professor, who has spent most of his life learning. Why, then, should we wonder that we are falling behind the rest of the world in scientific achievement?

One more major question should be examined in this bird's-eye view of progress: Where is this progress heading? What sort of future does this incredible progress have in store for us? Aldous Huxley tried to answer this question in the 1930's in his great book, *Brave New World*. In this grand fresco of the future, equality no longer exists. Society is carefully planned. People are manufactured in laboratories, baby factories, according to their future place in society. Only a few are left intact to fill the higher positions of society and a ten-member council directing the world. Only those ten have access to real knowledge of the past and the future, while the rest of the society is kept ignorant, fed on cheap, specially designed entertainment and a pleasure drug that keeps them satisfied and happy. The hero of the book, a reject of the system, his brain left intact by accident, rejects this society and chooses the reservation, where people live on the level of the Stone Age like animals in a zoo.

Is this the society toward which progress is relentlessly dragging us? Huxley reviewed progress in another book written almost 30 years later, and he stated that it is astonishing how close we have come to the situation described in his original novel. *Brave New World Revisited* is an eye-opening book.

Not everybody sees progress as a menace. Progress is sometimes heralded as the greatest good that has ever happened to mankind, and the negative side of it not only is not shown but is carefully veiled. Some people like life so much that they would even like to prolong it to eternity, if that were possible. A new branch of science was created to deal with the question of prolonging life: gerontology. One of its most prominent researchers, a woman scientist, said in a television interview not so long ago that she could imagine that about 150 years from now we would be able to solve the problem of eternal life. The irony of this proud statement is that she is old, hopelessly old. She spent her life seeking something to prevent aging, but apparently found none, because if she had, I believe she would have been the first to use it.

No, science won't be able to prolong life, I believe, not even an hour. The date of death is written in the genes, and no one will ever be able to alter it.

Summing up the dubious blessing of progress, a subject that thick books wouldn't be enough to analyze, we can safely say that it has brought forth more problems, more misery, than if we had let nature take control of our lives. The massive interference in nature's ways has created unsolvable problems for us. We are on the verge of killing our environment, while the happiness we chase doesn't get a bit closer. Life around us has speeded up so that it is hard to keep pace with it. Everything around us has become mobile. We no longer have a fixed point in our lives. We are alienated from each other, frustrated and lonely; often locked in the prisons our apartments or houses have become, because of crime in the streets; plagued with many new forms of sickness resulting from everyday stress, which slowly consumes our minds and increases the number of unstable people let loose on the streets. But perhaps psychology, the newly invented branch of science, is the medicine to give us comfort, some dubious hope in a hopeless situation.

10

PSYCHOLOGY AND ITS EFFECT ON OUR LIFE

We are living in the age of permissiveness. Our society is often called the permissive society. Very few people know, however, that permissiveness is the direct result of the application of psychological principles to our lives. Psychology is the science that studies man's behavior, while assuming that man is only an animal. Most basic scientific study in psychology is carried out on animals. The results are then carefully evaluated and applied to the most advanced mammal, man. No other science has affected our life as totally as psychology. It has affected social customs, moral standards, ethics, education, the social sciences, literature and art, and even religion. Today a generation has grown up under the influence of careful psychological manipulation, and the result is shown in all walks of life, even in the declining productivity in our factories. We are constantly bombarded with scientifically designed psychological attempts to influence our ways of thinking.

The side effects of progress—alienation, frustration, and loneliness—are the direct result of the incredible stresses of modern life. This kind of stress was unknown in previous ages, and perhaps man isn't designed to endure such pressure. Everything is in transition around us; there is no single fixed point in our lives. The result of this incredible stress is that almost everybody suffers from some sort of mental disorder. Many break down under the stress and join the ever-increasing number of mentally ill. The number of those unfortunate, permanently damaged people is rapidly growing. Our hospitals are full of them. As a matter of fact, there are more people in hospitals with mental illness than with all other sicknesses combined.

Psychology started about a hundred years ago with the noble goal of finding a cure for mental illness, of rescuing those living dead from the fatal illness of insanity. But this noble goal was soon forgotten when the psychiatrists discovered more profitable pastures, the curing of social illness, which affects mostly bored, rich people. Soon the couch was invented, where rich patients could confess their sins and desires and receive absolution from the polite voice of these new priests of atheism in the name of omnipotent science. The ancient pagan science of dream analysis was revitalized, and rich old ladies flocked to the waiting rooms of the psychiatrists, paying huge fees for their services. Many found salvation and comfort in these new temples, especially those who were torn between God's laws and their own desires. They were assured nothing is wrong about breaking the laws of God, since God doesn't exist anyway; they should feel free to live out their fantasies and should shed their guilty feelings. This was exactly what these patients wanted to hear; thus psychology soon climbed to the highest esteem among the rich, whose illness was in fact boredom. The incredible fees made it possible to further psychiatric research, to improve methods, and to exert influence over more and more people and larger segments of life. Applied psychology now is inseparable from modern life.

In a society where the most basic instinct, hunger, is satisfied, the emphasis shifted to the second most important instinct, sexuality, which directs the continuance of the race. One of the best-known founders of modern psychology, Freud, recognized the impact of the most basic instinct on man's life, and exploited it. All his theories are based on sexuality. Since sexuality is a subject that everybody is interested in, his theories soon became very popular. Freud taught that the suppression of sexual desires is wrong and is the cause of many mental disorders. Thus the laws forbidding the fulfillment of sexual desires are wrong and have to be done away with. His teaching slowly went into practice, and his greatest triumph can be seen in the victory of the sexual revolution sweeping through the world in the second half of our century. The result of it is well known, in the destruction of the family, which in turn will soon result in the destruction of society, since the family is the basis of society.

Freud did away with God's moral laws, the very fiber of social life, which lifted man above the level of the animals. The destruction of moral fiber made animals of men, successfully "proving" Darwin's theory that man is only another animal. It is interesting to note that Darwin shared the same obsession with sex that Freud had. One would be surprised at how large a role sexuality plays in Darwin's fundamental work, *The Origin of Species.* Darwin viewed sexuality as the main factor in natural selection. Freud's obsession with sex is incredible. Once he even asked his famous colleague Jung to help him to make his sexual theory into a dogma. "A dogma of what?" you may ask. The dogma of the new religion, atheism. But Jung, with a healthy skepticism, not only denied his help, but secretly despised Freud's obsession. As we know, Freud succeeded anyway, though he didn't live to see the triumph of his theory.

Men are lifted up above the level of animals by the knowledge of God, and religion regulates how we can be lords over our animal instincts. The difference between men and animals is that men are capable of overruling the instincts, which are the sole directors of animal life. It is quite natural that atheists, including Freud, who wants man to regress to the level of animals, conceive of religion and the concept of God as their enemies. Freud's hatred of religion had no bounds. He thought that religion was a collective neurosis, a mild form of mental illness, which should be cured. Little effort is needed to imagine what cure he proposed— free sex, of course, maybe in the form of group therapy.

Today, psychology is the same mixture of truth and lies as is Darwinism. While Darwin provided atheism with its second dogma—that nature, including man, was created not by God but by chance—Freud formulated the third dogma of atheism, that there is no such thing as a soul. He said that the concept of a soul is only the personification of dreams. Since long-deceased loved ones sometimes came back in dreams, this gave rise to the misconception that the soul is eternal. If there is no soul, then man is only another animal, just as Darwin taught. Man can be studied and manipulated just as animals can, and we can explain why man behaves as he does.

Psychology set out to understand the human mind. Its goal

was to be able to predict and manipulate human behavior. As we saw in Chapter 2, the human body is a complete universe in itself if we view it on the atomic level. So is the mind. We are not able to understand the many whys of a single building block of our body, a single DNA molecule. The body, like the mind, is built up of countless millions of molecules like DNA. The most simple model of the mind is so complicated that it indicates the impossibility of our ever understanding it. The mind has another interesting feature: the cells of the mind function from birth to death, unchanged. The human mind is the most advanced, most complicated matter in the universe. According to our beliefs, it is the dwelling place of the soul, the tool through which the soul directs the body, and through which it exists in this three-dimensional world. We are able to approach it in a general sense, to describe its main activities, but we will never be able to understand fully how it functions. To leave out the soul when describing the mind is like describing a car without mentioning the man who drives it. Why do the billions of atoms associate and function in the mind? What keeps them in place, working ceaselessly throughout a lifetime? Why is this set of atoms capable of reflecting on the universe, while other animals with somewhat similar minds are not able to do so? Who can answer these questions? We could ask many more, which will indicate still further that the task of understanding the human mind is impossible.

To abolish the concept of the soul is an oversimplification without foundation, just as is the simplistic approach to creation devised by Darwin. On the other hand, psychology contains many truths. Our body was taken from the animal kingdom, thus we share many things with the animals: instincts, reflexes, and automatic processes. The basic differences between animals and men is that, while the animals are not able to override instincts, we are. How to regulate the instincts is written in God's laws, the Ten Commandments, which we inherited from the Jews. These commandments are the basis of all law, upon which all societies must be built if they want to function. Psychology, however, disagrees with the usefulness of these laws. Psychology argues that the suppression of instincts, such as the sexual instinct, is basically wrong, that it will result in mental disorders, harming the personality of the individual. Psychology has declared war on these "inhuman" laws, astutely and persistently attacking them during the last hundred years, destroying their validity, and reeducating the public. The result is our permissive society, where sin is considered virtue, while virtue has become something to be ashamed of. God's laws are ousted from the schools, but our children are manipulated constantly with psychology. Freud has become the basis of sex education for the greater glory of a school system that has admittedly failed.

Psychology has successfully destroyed the moral fabric of society, pushing the individual back to the level of animals. The result is before our eyes: sexual revolution, unlimited pornography, widespread use of drugs, the crime wave, rape, sexual abuse of children, and incest. The lawlessness of the permissive society is destroying its very foundation: the family. Today, half of all marriages end in divorce, and soon more illegitimate children will be born than legitimate. And the end is nowhere in sight. Psychology is shaking the very foundations of society.

As we saw, psychology is far from its original goal. In the hands of atheists it has become a tool against God instead of the effective treatment of insanity. The mentally ill are forgotten completely. The few who still insist on the original goal feel psychology must share the blame for this gross neglect. Psychiatrists only confuse the picture with their divided opinions. Their real aim is to make money, not to treat illness.

Psychology is successful in manipulating the individual. It has abolished the laws of God and liberated the animal instincts in man. But there is an application of psychology more important than the manipulation of the individual: the manipulation of the whole society. This manipulation is often called propaganda. There are two major fields where mass manipulation is widely applied. One is the world of big business; the other is the world of politics. There is an outstanding book on that subject, probably the only one that dares to explore this forbidden field, Aldous Huxley's *Brave New World Revisited.* A more appropriate title might be *Applied Psychology.* In this book, Huxley examines the application of modern mind-control methods as they are applied by the totalitarian power to enslave the masses, to impose the will of a few on the whole society. He also explores the application of psychology in the business world.

Psychology is the basis of the consumer society. The essence of this new concept is that the consumer has to be persuaded, by means of various psychological methods to consume more than he really needs. Today's supersalesman applies a wide variety of psychological methods to achieve his goals, to convince the consumer he must buy more, thus promoting waste in a wholesale fashion. In a world of diminishing resources and exploding population, the idea of the consumer society is a contradiction in terms. While in most parts of the world many people don't have the bare necessities of life, a small part consumes and wastes most of what is produced.

Big corporations are now employing psychologists in large numbers. The task of these men is to explore human weaknesses, hidden fears, and desires, to find ways to appeal to them, and to exploit them for the greater profit of their employers. Human weaknesses are then linked with the product, placed in a carefully selected scene that is pleasing to the eyes, and transmitted to your living room through television commercials. Commercials are persuasions to buy certain products. But they seek to appeal, not to your reason, but to the subconscious; this is why constant repetition is so important. Even if you resist the commercial consciously, your resistance will be to no avail. When the time comes for you to choose between products in the supermarket, you will choose those that were advertised. Commercials aimed at youngsters are especially effective.

Psychology is a misleading word. It has religious overtones, since its root is the Greek word *psyche*, meaning "life," "spirit," or "soul," but psychology has nothing to do with religion; quite the contrary. This science is based on experiments conducted on animals. The observation of animal behavior provided psychologists with their basic laws. Such laws then can be applied to humans, since our body, including the mind, belongs to the animal kingdom. The soul is not the subject of psychological research. Psychology is basically intended to manipulate the animal in us. Such manipulation is similar to the process by which a disease manipulates our body. The foreign entity, a virus or a bacterium, wants to impose its will on the cells and eventually on the whole body, robbing it of its own functions and goals. If the body is not able to overcome the foreign presence, it will eventually die. The manipulation of the individual is a disease, but the manipulation of the whole society is an epidemic. It means that a few are able to impose their will on the whole society, contrary to its best interests. These days, methods have been developed by which a few atheists could subdue the whole world, robbing it of its freedom and imposing their will on it.

Hitler was the first to apply the modern methods of mass manipulation successfully. Using psychology, he was able to rob a whole nation of independent thought, the very basis of freedom, and to subject them to his own will. His success was possible because of new technical devices that had been invented, such as the radio, microphone, and film. Millions and millions were able to watch the carefully staged rallies and speeches without being physically present at them. Thus the effect was a lot wider than would have been possible in previous times. Thanks to the radio, the demagogic speeches were heard all over the country. These speeches were designed to appeal to the hidden desires and fears of the people, fears that were deeply seated in their subconscious minds. Hitler was able to touch everyone; he appealed to their sufferings, linked his appeal to the essentials of life, exploited their pride (which was at a low ebb after the defeat of World War I), and showed them a scapegoat, the Jews, as the source of their sufferings. Thus he manipulated the hidden fears and hopes of almost everybody. The suggestibility of the Germans at that time was especially high. The memory of the sufferings of the war, the chaos that followed it, and the sufferings caused by the Great Depression were all nerve-wracking, and Hitler presented himself as one who promised not only to end all this, but to provide superiority and prosperity beyond all imagining. Hitler carefully exploited the anxiety and fears of the masses, assailing them with stereotyped, constantly repeated slogans. This constant repetition finally succeeded in imprinting the desired idea in the minds of the German people.

Despite all this effort, Hitler didn't totally succeed. This may have been due to the primitive nature of his technical devices, or to the underdeveloped state of the psychological methods applied. Today, more perfect methods and devices like television open the possibility that a similar attempt might be more successful. Today not only the voice of the "master" but his picture can enter your living room, making him omnipresent. Psychological methods have been highly perfected since the Second World War. The more effective methods of brainwashing have been invented and applied; thus the possibility that a would-be dictator might succeed is a lot greater in our days.

Brainwashing is the most advanced form of applied psychology. It is based on the experiments of Ivan Pavlov, a Soviet scientist. He discovered the phenomenon by experimenting with dogs. Pavlov noticed that dogs subjected to prolonged physical or psychic stress exhibit, after a time, signs of a nervous breakdown. But before reaching the breaking point, their suggestibility is so heightened that new behavior patterns can be imprinted in their minds easily and ineradicably. These new behavior patterns are as strong as automatic reflexes. The only difference is that these new reflexes cannot be inherited, as could the other ones. This is why he called them conditioned reflexes. These new reflexes are automatic processes, too, independent of the conscious mind and located in the subconscious.

For this discovery Pavlov is heralded as the greatest Soviet scientist. His new discovery was immediately applied to humans, to the enemies of the state. Political prisoners were subjected to cruel pressure, both physical torture and psychological stress, and their communist captors were soon able to gain confessions from them. Those poor souls confessed to almost anything just to be rid of the torture.

One of the best examples of how such confessions can be gained by the application of the new method is the case of Cardinal Mindszenty. His iron will was broken during 14 days of torture, as he describes in his memoirs. He was beaten 14 consecutive nights, while he was deprived of sleep during the day. The physical torture was coupled with psychological duress, for mind-altering drugs were administered to him through his food. This method achieved its desired effect. After 14 days he was near a nervous breakdown. The boundaries between truth and lie slowly faded away, together with the strong will to resist at any cost. His memory became clouded, self-confidence vanished, lethargy and visions played tricks on him, and he had a growing conviction that all resistance was pointless. The torture was no longer bearable, and the body was ready to do anything to get rid of it. Thus he signed the false confession put before him, a confession that accused him of crimes he had never even thought of.

The case of Cardinal Mindszenty is a typical example of how the new psychological methods can be applied to an individual in the interest of the totalitarian state, of how they can be used to destroy the resistance of an iron-willed person. But destruction is not the only application of this new method; after all, the state has a very limited use for individuals who are nervous wrecks. The more important application of the new method is to create absolutely loyal individuals, propagandists of the new faith, the lower-level leaders of communism. The candidates for the new leadership are normal people who are conditioned to become fanatic leaders. The essence of this conditioning is the training camp, usually located in a remote area. The candidates are separated from their loved ones, their family and friends. They are made to do exhausting physical and psychic work. They are never left alone, and are encouraged to spy on each other; they are required to write and rewrite self-accusing autobiographies of their ignominious past; and they are told that failing the course will have dreadful consequences. All is designed to heighten their suggestibility as much as possible. In that state they are subjected to an intensive course in Marxism, which they must learn in order to succeed. Many of them break down during the course, but those who succeed emerge with new and ineradicable behavior patterns. A similar method is applied by the new sects to brainwash their victims. Many reports of the Moonies suggest that they employ the same methods. It is completely useless to enter into an argument with a person who has been brainwashed. Reason cannot prevail in the face of conditioned reflex, written deep in the subconscious.

Brainwashing, however, is not limited to the conditioning

of an individual. It can be applied with slight modifications to whole nations to make them accept "new truths." Such "new truths" were planted in the minds of whole Central European nations after the Second World War. These nations, newly acquired as colonies by the Soviet Union with the blessing of the Western powers, were subjected to collective brainwashing. After the sufferings endured during the war, the people of those nations were on the verge of a nervous breakdown. This heightened their suggestibility to a point where "new truths" could be imposed on them. This new truth was that, whether they liked it or not, they were in the hands of the communists, and all resistance was vain. This fact was emphasized by the presence of the cruel Red Army. The Western powers mildly insisted on free elections to let those nations decide on their future. Such elections were held, and although the people said an emphatic *No* to communism, this didn't alter their fate. The Western powers didn't have the will to enforce the clear decision of those unfortunate people, sold as slaves to the most cruel and inhuman power that ever existed on earth. Democratic forces were systematically shattered. The leading democratic figures were imprisoned or executed. Strategic lies are repeated by the radio, television, and the newspapers constantly. Opposing views or the truth can't be discussed, even in private, because one never knows who is a spy. People are conditioned from the cradle to the grave. Lies are accepted as truth, sometimes even by those who know positively that they are lies, because of the constant repetition. The media are the best tool for mind manipulation, and the media are owned by the communist state. Whoever controls the media is able to control the minds of the people. Through mechanization of the media, psychology has become the sharpest weapon in the hands of dictators.

Huxley expressed his fear for the fate of Western-type democracies, which, according to him, are becoming more and more subject to this new method of manipulation. The essence of the Western-type democracy is a well-informed, educated public that is able to govern itself. Educating the public is a hard task and is increasingly being replaced by methods of mass manipulation. Instead of educating voters, both parties employ techniques similar to the methods used to sell goods. Candidates are carefully wrapped in an image supposed to be pleasing to the public; then this image is merchandised, using scientific psychological methods to sell it to the people. This process doesn't appeal to the reason of the voters, and genuine issues are seldom discussed. Instead, politicians seek to appeal to people's weaknesses, content merely to manipulate and exploit those hidden desires.

The present situation in the big cities is equivalent, in a sense, to conditioning. People suffer intensively from unchecked crime, which causes constant fear, alienation, and loneliness, symptoms that lead to a heightened suggestibility. Besides that, many voluntarily take mind-altering drugs. Such a crowd soon will be suggestible to "new truths," which might promise law and order, a peaceful life again, under some form of dictatorship.

In previous ages, society made tremendous efforts to help the individual to overcome his animal instincts. All laws and religious education tried to lift man above the level of the animals, to help him to become a bit more human every day, to strengthen his divine nature by controlling the animal instincts. In our age, however, this trend has been reversed. From the cradle to the grave we are subject to constant and repeated psychological manipulation, not appealing to our potential strengths, but exploiting our animal weaknesses, our worst part, the subconscious instincts, the animal in us. This makes it impossible for the soul to overcome the animal and to lift man closer to his supernatural destiny. Impersonal forces, like invisible viruses, manipulate our lives, and yet we wonder why our world is sick and driven to despair, willingly subjecting itself to the will of the enemy, whose only goal is to drive God out of the earth, and to destroy us with Him.

Psychology is a very destructive force, both on the personal and on the social level. As its founder, Freud, stated, psychology perceives religion and God as its main targets, its chief enemies. Its goal is to bring man to the rank of the animals. The methods devised and used by psychology are so strong that almost no defense is possible against them. Such methods employed to bring down mankind will soon have the desired effect, the breakdown of mankind and its willing acceptance of a new, heavy yoke, a new form of slavery that is already in effect in large parts of the world. Hitler didn't succeed in his time, but today it is possible that a would-be dictator might succeed in enslaving all of mankind all over the world. The tools are ready; they await only the man who would use them.

Does all this mean that psychology is evil?

No, far from it. But even the most innocent thing can become evil in the hands of evil men. The hidden forces of our nature discovered by psychology can be put to use to lift up mankind just as effectively as they are now used to sink men in a swamp of sin. Psychology could give us powerful tools for overcoming our weaknesses; it could lift us to unknown heights, unimaginable before. It could make us more human, closer to the ideal state, in which the soul is lord over the body. Methods discovered by psychology could be used to strengthen the good in us and to reform those individuals such as criminals who are not able to overcome their animal nature, their weaknesses. It is interesting to note that while psychology saturates our lives, it is not permitted to enter into the world of prisons, where it could be put to real use to reform hard-core criminals. The prisons, the supposed reforming institutions, do not use psychological methods to imprint new conditioned reflexes on the minds of criminals so that they will not offend society anymore. Psychology could be used to impose the will of the good over the bad, not the opposite, as is going on now.

But today psychology is used by the enemies of God, and not too many people are aware that the enemies of God are the enemies of mankind as well.

11

WHAT'S WRONG WITH SCIENCE?

In the previous chapters I have attempted to give a bird's-eye view of the different branches of science. Mankind has learned a lot during the past few centuries, but there is a lot more to learn than what we know at this time. Some scientists proclaim that we have reached the peak of our knowledge. Does that mean we now know everything? Certainly not. But they just may be right. It is possible that we have reached the limit of our ability to penetrate deeper into the vast ocean of knowledge, although we still are only knee-deep in this ocean. It is possible that we have reached the limit of our ability.

The ultimate conclusion of modern physics, the uncertainty principle, applies to all our knowledge. Depending upon what part of science we are talking about, this uncertainty increases a hundredfold, or, to use a more precise term, by powers of ten. This uncertainty, however, isn't advertised. Quite the contrary. If the uncertainty about a particular branch of science increases, the propagandists of that branch become louder and louder, in an attempt to shout down any possible opposition. This attitude originated in the basic philosophy of science: materialism and atheism.

The reason why science embraced this philosophy has a historical and a logical basis. Science deals with the material world; thus it is logical that it has to limit its scope to those aspects of the world that can be perceived by our senses. Materialism thus came naturally to science. This focus was a basic agreement, even in the past, when science was an infant, the daughter of theology and philosophy. While science dealt with the material world, theology dealt with the supernatural world, and philosophy existed in between the two as a balance. The equilibrium lasted about a thousand years, until science suddenly started to grow and the balance was lost.

Our information about the natural world exploded. Old values changed from one day to the next. But the truth of this new reality wasn't as obvious then as it is now. Strangely enough, observational evidence didn't clearly favor either theory of the solar system; it was hard to choose between Ptolemy and Copernicus. It is the same in our days with many new ideas. For example, it is quite obvious to me that the center of the sun, and consequently of the stars, can't be the place of the energy-generating process. Energy generation must occur on the boundary between the enclosed energy and the material shell, not far below the surface of the stars. But all accepted astronomical theories are based on Eddington's widely accepted model, which places an atomic reactor in the center of the stars and we are stuck with further development. How can one prove or disprove this? The observational evidence that prompted me to change my opinion is not sufficient to change all of science. Anyway, science has a built-in inertia that works against sudden changes. The Voyager programs clearly proved how uncertain is our knowledge of even our closest neighbors. There is a wide gap between observation and theory, even in this case, where our knowledge of astronomy must be the most accurate, since the distances are negligible compared with distances to other stars. This must mean to any thinking person that gaps must exist between our theories and reality in many other cases. But no such statement surfaces anywhere. It should be obvious that if our theory about the members of the solar system was wrong, then other theories about the sun may prove to be wrong, too. But no, any such idea is anathema.

The acceptance of a new idea, such as the new hypothesis about the interior of the sun, could bring about a revolution more severe than the Copernican one. It would mean that most books would have to be rewritten. Many idols, idols so dear to mediocre minds, would suddenly fall. Many would have to admit that they were wrong in creating obstacles to change. But scientific revolutions do not work that way. First, the believers in the old theories have to die out, and the new generation must gradually come to believe in the necessity of a change. The acceptance of a new idea takes time, but it comes nevertheless.

It was the same in the time of Copernicus. The old values of science were so nicely interwoven with theology, the picture appeared so perfect, that when it was threatened by the new reality the majority of scientists felt endangered by the new thought and turned to theology for protection. Unfortunately, they got it. The new thought and its representatives soon were attacked from every side. Amidst the fierce battle, scientists didn't ask who it was who wanted to help them in this fight, so long as they were willing to give aid. Atheists seized this opportunity and lent a helping hand to the new thought. The rich representatives of atheism soon became the only mentors of science. The alliance between science and atheism thus dates back to the puberty of science. It is a marriage made, not in heaven, but rather in hell, blessed by Satan himself. Science got its reward. It was free to explore; scientists became famous; and the fame of science overshadowed the fame of its parents, theology and philosophy. As a matter of fact, both became dwarfs beside overinflated science. But a price tag was attached.

Under the new master, atheism, no restrictions were placed on scientific exploration. Scientists could dig wherever they wanted—if they obeyed one slight rule, that they leave the explanation of the results to those competent thinkers who knew how to use them properly in the service of atheism against its main enemies, religion and God. This appeared to scientists to be an unimportant aspect. The important thing was that they be free to dig. The digging was the source of the excitement and the satisfaction. The best example of this is today's scientists under communist rule. Most of them disagree with the communist ideology, but they serve it anyway because the built-in urge to do research, to explore, is stronger than the consideration whom they serve in doing so. This urge is almost an instinct, an unquenchable fire, constantly pressing them to go further, to explore, to discover new things.

In the early stages of the development of science, there was competition between schools of thought. This competition, however, vanished over the centuries. Without competition and healthy criticism, science became very one-sided. New discoveries went on unchecked. This created an atmosphere in which scientists were even tempted to cheat, either to advance more quickly or just for material reward. One of the most prominent examples of scientific cheating is a Soviet biologist, Olga Lepisinskaja. She claimed during the 1940's that she had created new living matter, new cells. Of course it turned out a hoax, the result of cheating, but for decades her "breakthrough" was taught in the Soviet Union and behind the Iron Curtain as a major proof against the necessity of God in the creation. I am sure that her breakthrough still lingers in atheist literature, even in the West, since the fact that she had cheated didn't get as much publicity as did her great "result."

But not only communist scientists tend to be cheaters. In the mid-1970's the *New York Times* had to deal with the subject, after two scandals became public knowledge. In the article, "Even for Scientists There is a Temptation to Cheat," Edelson mentions two cases where scientists were caught cheating. I do not wonder about the cheating parapsychologist, but cheating in cancer research is a lot more serious. The author of the article tries to explain cheating by the tremendous pressure on researchers to succeed. This creates an atmosphere that forces them to win at any price in order to be able to get ahead in the scientific world.

You may suppose that scientists have only one motive: to get closer to the truth. Most great scientists, of course, have pursued this goal, but this isn't the case with all scientists. I have read on many occasions that today's scientists are no longer interested in the absolute truth. At first I didn't want to believe this, but later I was convinced that unfortunately it is true. Today's scientists suffer from myopia. They are shortsighted specialists, who no longer see their field as a whole. They see only small details, which must fit into the puzzle whose framework was established in the last century by militant atheists. They are specialists. This means that they excel in only a small area, and ceaselessly dig for minute details. If you look at the achievements of today's Nobel laureates, you will notice that they have usually been cited for minute research. Such geniuses as Einstein no longer are considered to be scientists; they never get any awards.

Thor Heyerdahl in his book *Kon-Tiki* describes the specialists of our time as ones who "limit their own scope in order to be able to dig for more details. Modern research demands that every special branch dig in its own hole. It's not usual for anyone to sort out what comes up out of the holes and try to put it all together." I think Heyerdahl caught the spirit of modern science: specialization. Specialization is necessary for many reasons. One of them is the increasing price of research. The other reason is that this method allows us to gain deeper knowledge. But it seems to me that we have gone a bit too far in this direction. The time is ripe to put together the bits and pieces that have come up from the individual holes. Many of them no longer fit into the old atheistic pattern, and loudly cry out for a new framework, a new natural philosophy.

Heyerdahl, however, was not quite correct. There are thinkers who from time to time pick up the pieces that come out of the holes. It is, of course, another question whether or not they are able to do the job. In most cases, evidence that does not fit into the atheistic philosophy is simply ignored or thrown away, so that no one is disturbed by unnecessary doubts. One of such "certified" thinkers is Carl Sagan, who works in the fields of geology and astronomy. He is a direct descendant of the last century's militant atheists. For him, Darwinism is no longer a theory, but a fact, and to explain the universe we don't need God at all. In his television series and book with the same title, "Cosmos," he proclaims our faint ideas of the universe as proven facts; yet he does this at a time—unfortunately for him—when our knowledge of our nearest neighbors is collapsing as the result of the Voyager programs.

It seems to me that the basic requirement for a scientist to become an officially recognized thinker is the open confession of the faith: atheism. Without that no one can be certified as a thinker. A self-appointed thinker will suffer the fate of Velikovsky, who was ridiculed, refuted, and cast out of science because he dared to question some dogmas of atheism. He presented and proved a different view than the officially accepted Darwinism, thus rendering it nonsense. He proved that Darwinism is anything but fact, and reality is entirely different from Darwin's theory. Furthermore, he successfully disproved the theory of Lyell about slow change. He dared to believe in the Bible. He took the story of the flood literally, successfully welding together ancient legends and geological discoveries. His proofs are irrefutable, but all this did not avail, for his "openminded" and "objective" opponents, clinging to their own erroneous beliefs, shouted him down loudly, not even considering that he might have some truth on his side. Modern science is more dogmatic than the Catholic Church ever was. He also violated an unwritten law of science, that every new thought has to be judged first by fellow scientists; in scientific matters it is prohibited to appeal to the public over the heads of scientists before gaining their approval.

One must go through official training, called education, before one may become a scientist. This training in our days is aimed at producing specialists. The professors themselves are specialists. But in such an environment a would-be genius is destined to be lost. Geniuses have a special brain, not necessarily interested in detailed studies, which are the basis of today's scientific research. The most excellent example of this is Einstein, who was considered by his teachers to be a below-average student, whose professional future was questionable. Education in a sense is brainwashing. Those students whose brains can be easily washed are rewarded with good grades most of the time. Such students believe everything that is taught them by the teacher. Those who have questions, who doubt some part of what they have heard, are a lot more difficult, but some of them may be geniuses, who, with healthy doubts, could advance science. Of course, this is only the exception, not the rule, since geniuses occur only once in a hundred years. To be a genius requires a lot more than a doubting mind. Education in our days unfortunately includes indoctrination in atheism. Atheistic views are freely presented in the schools in the name of secularism; but religion, the opposite viewpoint, is excluded, and schools are not even permitted to mention it. I doubt that this is democratic. It seems to me, rather, to be the dictatorship of atheism.

Future scientists are selected from the most eminent students, who show a particular interest in detailed, specialized studies. Such students first become assistants to the professor, helping him on his own research projects. Can you imagine that a professor with a strong atheistic conviction would select as his assistant a student who dared to question openly the dogmas of atheism? For example, that a professor of biology would select someone who said, "I don't believe in Darwinism, and I have a creationist view"? Or a candidate for psychology who believed that man has an eternal soul? I believe the answer is no in both cases, unless the candidate keeps his convictions to himself and openly acknowledges the views of his superior. Let us suppose that he plans to do research of his own to prove his views, and since he is young he has time to publish them later when he has established his own name. When finally he reaches his goal and becomes chairman of the department, he decides that this is the right moment to reveal the truth. But he is obliged to present his opinions first to his fellow scientists, who also have atheistic views inherited from their predecessors. If he still holds his views and wants to present them to his colleagues, he commits scientific suicide. His reward will be ridicule, at best, or deep silence and regret that he apparently went insane during his long years of study. And if he has not the talent to appeal to the public over the heads of his colleagues, he is likely, after a bitter life, to carry his thoughts to his grave.

This is a vicious circle, from which there is no escape. Atheism gained the upper hand over science long ago. There is no way that atheism will let go of science without a battle. Atheists reserve the right to explain the universe around us, and no one is permitted to question their explanations. This is the famous openmindedness and objectivity of atheist science. One may ask: Do you see a conspiracy behind all this? I suspect one, but that is not the subject of this book. It would be interesting, however, to retrace the path by which atheist scientists gained total power over universities that were established by Christianity long, long ago. In our time, universities all over the world have become the headquarters of the fight against religion and God.

The motor behind any progress is competition. In the early stages of scientific development, such competition existed. Different schools of thought saw reality in different lights. This competition, however, vanished over the centuries. Scientists everywhere accepted a general set of values, a unified philosophy of science. Science has developed toward specialization, and the basis of scientific research is no longer examined; it is taken for granted. In our days we have piled up so many details that no longer fit into the pattern of old values that this basis of science has become questionable. But questioning it is not allowed. Any such questioning is considered to be an attack on science and meets a violent reception, as witness Velikovsky. From an open-minded science, one would rightfully expect that a new thought would at least get some consideration, the realization that it might be true or partially true, especially in the case of Velikovsky, who presented unimpeachable proofs that he was right. But no one considered them. Why was he immediately shouted down? Didn't he deserve a hearing, at least? No, because he was a heretic, who dared to deviate from the official atheist dogmas.

In previous chapters I pointed out just what might be the basis of a revision of natural philosophy. The very basis of this philosophy is the law that the natural laws we have uncovered on earth are valid all over the universe. Our increased knowledge has rendered this false assumption obsolete. It is simply not true if we recognize how unique the state of matter on earth is in the universe. Some laws of physics may have universal application, but in most cases the constants in the laws show that they are only extreme cases of possible universal law. The newly observed rings of Saturn are an excellent example of how limited the application of our laws is. If the rings of Saturn followed our known laws, they wouldn't be there at all. They would have fallen into the planet a long time ago. These rings point out another possible error of ours. The currently accepted theory of the origin of the solar system supposes such rings around the orbits of the planets to be the first stage of their evolution. It is said that these rings contracted by gravitation to form the planets. Why, then, don't Saturn's rings condense into moons? Apparently our presumption is wrong, but this doesn't bother the representatives of this false theory, such as Sagan, who is so sure of his ideas that in a religiously charged tone he teaches America, "We don't need a God to understand the unverse!"

The state of matter on earth is so unique that in itself it is enough to contradict the universal validity of laws concerning it. The possible extension of these laws to the universe suffers a major setback if we accept or even consider a universe built mostly of energy. The laws of energy are beyond our comprehension, possibly forever. This energy is invisible to us, since it is confined to the stars and the interior of atomic particles. These few ideas should be sufficient to humble our scientists and to put science back where it belongs. Science today is artificially inflated and no longer reflects reality. The time has arrived for it to step down from the clouds, to shed its false notions, and to reoccupy its natural place between theology and philosophy.

But who can undertake the task of sobering science up? Certainly not the universities under atheist control. The only imaginable institutions left to consider are the few remaining Christian universities. They must revive, and begin to provide healthy competition for the atheist interpretation of science. But there are many obstacles, and the greatest among them is specialization. Universities must provide room for the education of thinkers beside specialists, and it is debatable whether a specialist can be considered a scientist at all. I have the impression that a more appropriate term would be *scientific worker*. Only those who can come up with new ideas to further our knowledge, who can put together the bits and pieces of research dug out by the specialists, should be considered scientists.

The atmosphere of present-day science is hostile to the emergence of thinkers. The chairs of the universities are occupied by specialists, who in turn select for scientific careers candidates capable of specialized, minute research. The mind of the thinker works differently than the mind of a specialist. The thinker always wants to see broad expanses of the field in order to uncover relationships—exactly the opposite of specialized research, which is concerned mainly with small, limited numbers of details. A specialist has to have the ability to split hairs. For the thinker, this is not only boring; most of the time it is impossible.

In today's scientific world, the basis of science is taken for granted. Going back to reexamine this basis, it is not only not appreciated, most of the time it is discouraged. The way a new generation of thinkers can be produced is just the opposite. People must be encouraged to reexamine the basis of a whole science, carefully scrutinizing its fundamental values. This could be done by giving this sort of task as an option for Ph.D. candidates. Such a method wouldn't produce geniuses in wholesale fashion, but there would be a few who through this opportunity would become thinkers, and some of them might prove to be geniuses. During the last century, in Europe, international competitions were held for scientists to attempt to solve a problem. Many great names of science were recognized through participation in such competitions. Today this has been replaced by international symposiums, which have become forums where specialists can present their latest findings. The nineteenth-century competitions were held, not only in science, but also in philosophy, and allowed many great philosophers to rise to fame and to find financial support for further work.

Such competitions calling for the reexamination of a branch of science could result in many new ideas. Besides, they would be able to eliminate many misconceptions burdening science today. Many branches of science are burdened unnecessarily with atheistic ideas. There is a good example in psychology of just how beneficial a reexamination of old values can be: Jung reviewed the thoughts of alchemy and found them very useful. Of course, this doesn't mean that I agree with his findings, but such research could trigger new thoughts, and it would help to clarify many misconceptions. Velikovsky did the same. He reviewed theories about the Pleistocene era and found that many gaps existed. He then successfully welded his new findings and ancient legends, and thus came to a more logical conclusion than anyone before him. For me, it proved very fruitful to rethink the early history of the earth in the light of theories concerning the origin of the solar system. This yielded a complete new line of hypotheses in astronomy. Of course that line needs to be developed further, but without hope of recognition, the task is difficult.

The present state of science cries out for new ideas. In most branches of science, we have reached a dead end, and this is due to the misguided direction given by the atheistic-materialistic natural philosophy adopted by science in the last century.

Today this atheistic philosophy is like a straitjacket restricting the further development of science.

Unfortunately, even theology and philosophy were swept away by the atheistic trend. Philosophy is giving out very disturbing, dissonant sounds with its new existentialist tendencies. Art is also headed in this direction and inclines more toward insanity than beauty. Theologians fall into this web, too. They wanted to reconcile the idea of God with science, but instead of converting atheists, they were themselves converted and lost their own faith. Since then many of them have spread their own disbelief, sometimes misleading even those who were not affected by, or infected with, the virus of false knowledge. They became wolves dressed in sheep's skin.

For example, theologians could point out how marvelous the ancient conception of the vaults of heaven was, a conception that was ridiculed during the past few centuries, until science was able to prove their existence. Science recognized the protective shields surrounding the earth only during the second half of this century (1958). Science calls them the Van Allen belts, after their discoverer, but they are the same as the vaults of heaven. These belts are so important that without them life wouldn't be able to exist on earth. They are the protective shields God placed above us. Isn't it marvelous that even the despised men of the Bible knew about them, but the enlightened atheists of the last century did not?

Countless similar confirmations await, and others that still appear to be superstition may represent more advanced knowledge. I have pointed out that Genesis is not in error in saying that apparently light was created twice, on the first and the fourth days. It is only because of our ignorance that we still cannot decipher that coded message. This can be viewed as proof that the universe was created from pure energy gradually, from energy proceeding from the mouth of God, if you wish. Reexamination of the values of ancient thought could be very inspiring, and could pay high dividends by opening up whole new realms of reality. But atheism, with its negative outlook, limits the scope of science today. This is why the Christian universities, if they are free from atheistic views, can be seen as the best equipped today to free science from this bondage. To do so, however, they must shake off the atheistic influence, the depressing mentality caused by the loudly proclaimed victory of atheist science over theology. But it wasn't a victory, anyway. The war is not yet over, and victory is not a negative thing; it always prefers the positive, which is represented by us. We Christians must pull ourselves together, and then the victory, the real one, will be ours. Our philosophy is positive, not restricted like that of materialism and atheism. We should be able to move science out of its present stalemate.

Science today feels the need for some reconciliation with the idea of the supernatural and God, but it is searching for this in a dangerously mistaken direction. This is why parapsychology, ESP, black magic, and witchcraft have gained recognition in the universities. This tendency is the direct result of atheism, which has created a vacuum that is being filled by satanic ideas. But this isn't the direction that will lead science out of its problems; instead, it will create even more problems than we have now. It will only multiply the number of lies, and will bury truth even deeper. The only way science can emerge from its present depression is to be reconciled with God and the true religion. In this way it could become more fruitful.

Today's atheist science tends to despise the scientific results of previous ages. The history of science is dealt with very briefly, mostly in negative terms; only the obstacles to progress, mainly religion, are examined. The evolution of ideas is neglected, since if properly shown it might hint that our present achievements will become obsolete in turn. Scientists also tend to forget that without the thinkers of the past who explored the various paths of science, we wouldn't be here. The despised and ridiculed Christian scientists explored the territory of science, eliminating unproductive areas and enabling us to focus our attention on those paths that would yield results. Thus they provided the basis for today's development. Only Christianity can expand the mind of men to receive further knowledge. If this wasn't so, then science would have developed on some other cultural ground, such as Hinduism or Islam. But this wasn't the case, despite the fact the basic ideas of science were widely known to many other cultures. As we know, none of them was able to advance knowledge. One of the most clear-cut examples is the Chinese. The Chinese were advanced in medicine and in many other aspects of science; for example, they knew about explosives. They also had a highly unified culture that supported scientific development, a culture undisturbed for thousands of years. Yet science was destined to develop in barbarous, dark Europe, with its Christianity as the "greatest obstacle" to scientific development, or so the atheists accuse.

There is a definite connection between science and the enemy of God, Satan. It cannot be an accident or mere coincidence that the "Fall of Man" is so closely connected with knowledge. Satan promised to our ancestors that if they ate the apple of knowledge they would be like gods. This turned out to be a lie, and caused the greatest disappointment in human history. Science today says something similar. If we deny the existence of God, we instantly become the most advanced beings in the universe or, in other words, we are gods. In Paradise this turned out to be a lie, and nothing has changed since: it is a lie today, too, even if it isn't as self-evident and hasn't been immediately followed by punishment. Buying this lie resulted in the downfall of man, the loss of eternal life and a happy relationship with God. The difference today is only that the punishment is delayed until after the short life on earth—or might it be coming in the form of an atomic war?

It is hardly an accident that science developed on Christian soil. The present-day "miracles of science" represent the strongest possible temptation for mankind to abandon God. It gives us false security, even "proof" of our greatness, which cannot tolerate any other being above us. Such a temptation clearly serves the purposes of the enemy of God. Some scientific writers, such as Von Daniken, tried to prove that new scientific discoveries were and are inspired by supernatural forces. He mentions Kepler as an example. In one of his books Kepler described a dream in which he was taken to outer space and saw the entire solar system, which he later described. Some analysts of the controversial phenomenon of UFOs claim that these supposedly supernatural forces exercise control over men's minds. These and many similar cases strongly suggest that there is external interference in the development of scientific thought. If this is true, the scientists, though they are extraordinary people, are only tools in the hands of greater forces, who shape life on earth as they want to.

Nothing is wrong with knowledge itself. It is fundamentally wrong, however, for science to lend itself to atheists to be used against God and religion. When science is so used, it steps out of its own role, assuming the roles of theology and philosophy and thus becoming the foundation of a new religion: atheism. The god of this new religion sometimes disguises himself as chance, or a false law of nature, but he is revealed in the newest branches of science: parapsychology, ESP, and black magic, through which he wants to reestablish his own old cults, which flourished in the childhood of mankind. One does not have to dig too far to discover the identity of this new god, who is Satan himself in a new role.

He is the one who helped us develop science. He inspired the invention of the printing press, so that it would be ready when it was needed to tear the Church apart. He is the one who gives us from time to time more perfect weapons to kill each other. He inspired scientists to invent the ultimate weapon, which enables a few of his loyal servants to eliminate more than half of mankind in mere hours. He is the one who helped to invent more and more perfect devices to avert our attention from God, to distract us in every conceivable way, and finally to lead us astray. He is the one who wants to fill our empty hearts with his own cults: witchcraft and black magic.

But let us hope that mankind will soon awake from this hypnotic dream and not let itself be fooled any longer. More and more, real scientists recognize the absurdity of the atheist view of life that dominates science. The tide is turning, the revival of faith is on its way. Many will see the day when science renounces atheism and turns back to God. Then science will flourish again beyond all expectation. God, not Satan, is the real source of all knowledge. Satan possesses vast knowledge, but he is only a reflection, or more properly only the shadow, of his Creator, God. He is like the moon, reflecting the rays of the sun.

12

WHERE IS GOD IN THIS VASTLY EXPANDED UNIVERSE?

In past ages it was simpler to imagine God. Earth was then the center of the universe; the stars were only lamps to help night travelers; above the vaults of heaven were the spheres populated by the choirs of angels; and in the highest sphere sat God, the King of the universe. The earth was for humans, while the interior of the earth was believed to be for the fallen angels and was called hell. This crystal-clear, logical, understandable picture was suddenly shattered like a mirror in the new scientific discoveries. The psychological shock was so great that some theologians still seem unable to overcome it.

The universe has vastly expanded since the first discoveries, and we no longer find a place or a need for the Creator. It is interesting to note, however, that the spherical conception of the universe is still with us, although on an enlarged scale. The universe of Einstein is a sphere; infinity results from the curvature of space. The modern concept of the universe also uses spheres; although we talk, rather, about lenslike shapes, the essence is the same. Our galaxy, it is said, is only a part of a supergalaxy, also in a lenslike shape, which in turn is part of a larger megagalaxy built up of super galaxies, and we don't know with certainty that that is where it all ends. Since the universe is infinite, maybe Einstein was right and ultimately it ends as a sphere. If this is so, then wherever the material universe ends, the supernatural spheres must start, just as St. Thomas Aquinas imagined it. The difference is only that the boundary of the spheres has receded.

As we saw, it is very hard to escape from the spherical theory. Almost all entities in the universe show this spherical form. Is it a correct reflection of reality or is it only a limitation in our way of thinking? Who can answer that? The truth is that we possess very little observational evidence that might allow us to arrive at real knowledge about the nature of the infinite universe. Most of our theories are hypotheses only. God is positively above this material universe. To search for Him with scientific methods devised to test the unique matter around us is more than foolish. God is not matter; He cannot be found in the material universe.

The question then arises: If God is not in this material universe, then where is He? St. Thomas Aquinas made the last attempt to answer this question, but, as we know, he failed with Ptolemy, since he based his system on the since-outdated earth-centric conception. But did he really fail? Was the Ptolemaic concept so essential to his theory? Or, despite its wrong basis, was his theory not a splended guess at higher reality, the work of a genius who guessed the existence of dimensions long before the concept was introduced into science? I believe it was, but the primitive minds of the atheists of the last century weren't able to grasp the higher meaning of his theory. They saw his masterpiece only in the light of the failed Ptolemaic system, which was only one, and not even the basic, aspect of the theory of St. Thomas. Dimensions were discovered only later by Rhineman, and the concept started to catch on only in our time.

If we accept this explanation for the theory of St. Thomas, then we need not even touch it; in itself it is perfect and beyond possible improvement. (Here I must mention that I'm not familiar with modern Thomist philosophy, thus I may be echoing the thoughts of some recognized great philosopher who has come to the same conclusion.) The only thing we can do with this perfect theory is to translate it into modern scientific language. A rough sketch of such a translation follows.

The highest possible dimension in this new universe is reserved for God. Any attempt to define it by number is meaningless and, moreoever, unimportant. Below this dimension are the angels, who occupy the dimensions between God and man. The number of these dimensions is also unimportant, since we won't be able to acquire real knowledge of them. These angelic beings populate the universe, possibly. As a matter of fact, the universe as a whole exists in the fourth dimension. I have an impression that what we see as an expanding universe is only a pulsation, but this pulsation will not go to the supposed extremes, either to contract until the death of matter or to expand without end. It is simply an oscillation. In this universe man is unique with his three-dimensional existence and two-dimensional thoughts. This simply means that in this form we don't have eternal life, we don't exist in time. But this wasn't always so. In the beginning, our ancestors were created by God to be capable of eternal life, like the other four-dimensional creatures who now may populate the universe.

The Fall of Man resulted in the loss of eternal life. Death, with its senseless circle, entered our lives. This, however, will not be a circle of reincarnation until the end of time. After death, men will be able to regain their lost status according to their performance on earth. This possibility was opened up for us by Jesus Christ on the cross. The belief that death is not the end is so deeply rooted in the mind of mankind that it can be found everywhere, even in the past among the most primitive people. Whenever and wherever men lived in the distant past or in present times, even in complete isolation on the most primitive level, this thought occupies the center of their beliefs. Only modern pagans try to discredit it, very unsuccessfully.

We don't know exactly how we lost the fourth dimension, but nevertheless it is a fact. Whosoever is born must die. To deny the possibility of life after death is not progress in thinking, not the result of increased knowledge, but simply a step back to the ignorance of the animals. Each set of myths about the Fall of Man knows not only that men were subject to this degrading experience or curse of God, but that the whole planet earth was, too. Thus life on earth—as we know—must be a unique phenomenon in the universe. This, however, doesn't mean that no other form of life exists in the universe. As scientists point out, there are millions of planets in our galaxy that must be inhabitable by life forms similar to us. Thus it is possible that those planets are indeed inhabited, but by a different form of life. This life form may somewhat resemble us, but may exist on higher dimensions, at least in the fourth dimension, where those beings don't know death.

We try desperately to communicate with someone outside earth. We ceaselessly send signals, such as radio waves, based on our manner of communicating. But no answer has been received so far. It is quite imaginable that beings in the higher dimensions know of us anyway, but don't want to communicate with us. They must know that a prison island exists in the universe where people are subject to death as a punishment and exist in the lowest possible form of life. Our means of communication are foreign to them. They communicate by telepathy; thus they don't need any device to understand each other. We had to invent devices to improve our limited ability to communicate or to change place, which is the direct result of our lower status.

We may suppose that beings above our dimensions populate the universe. St. Thomas divided the angelic realm into three categories. I think it is quite possible that these three categories represent three different dimensions. Angels in the lowest category populate the universe. It is possible that they have leaders belonging to a dimension one step higher. If we apply our newly acquired knowledge to the universe, we may suppose that these angels have a head angel on a dimension still one step higher, who directs the life of a galaxy. The heads of the galaxies perhaps form a universal council that reports directly to God. Of course this new picture can be further elaborated, but I doubt we can arrive at real knowledge in this limited form. Besides, this knowledge is not ours to know. If we think in dimensions, we can approach the mystery of the Trinity. The Godhead occupies the highest possible dimension. In that dimension, only three persons exist; this is why we say in the profession of faith that Jesus is "one in being with the Father." The possibilities of this highest dimension are such that these three persons are perfectly equal, in complete harmony, unable to misunderstand or contradict each other; thus they act as one. Needless to say, all this is nothing but fantasy, but perhaps it is closer to the truth than any previous imagination, which is also far from real knowledge, since we have no idea just what life or existence in the higher dimensions could mean. The secrets of the universe and its real nature are not ours to know; our limited minds cannot even approach them.

Actually, we can't imagine a life even in the next, the fourth, dimension. Our body was degraded by God's curse, which probably meant a structural change. Imagine how different life on earth would be if at least our leaders were from a dimension one step higher, from the fourth dimension, which would mean that such a leader would have eternal life. Many miseries of history that were the result of human weakness and the imperfection of leaders could have been avoided. But relax, we are heading in exactly this direction.

Our Christian faith offers us hope. The sins of Adam and Eve pushed us into this lower dimension, but the sentence was not for eternity. As a matter of fact, God immediately promised that the punishment would end in time. We are even considered for parole through the merit of Jesus Christ, the second person of the Godhead, who loved us so much that through His incarnation He shared our humanity, this lowest form of life in the universe, to reconcile us with the Father. Through His most cruel death He lifted our sins and purchased for us the freedom of choice. This love didn't end with His death. He assured us that He will prepare a place for us where we can be with Him forever. This will be a unique place in the universe. We are destined to regain not only our previous status but much more. Those who succeed in following Him in this life will be the sons of the living God, the Most High, a status higher than the highest angels have. How pitiable are those unfortunates who fail to grasp this limitless possibility awaiting us, and sell their souls for nothing.

To understand better just what a special status is prepared for us, let's look at an example. In a corporate structure, the ladder usually goes as follows: the highest-ranking officer is the head of the company, after him usually come the vice-presidents, then the heads of the departments, and later the branch leaders. But in many companies there is a special place for specialists. They do not belong to the departments, and they usually report directly to the president. This is one of the best possible independent positions within a corporation. Jesus promised us this sort of special status in the universe. Because He himself will be our "boss," we are not going to be under the supervision of even the highest-ranking angels. Isn't this the greatest possibility man ever can grasp? Compare it with the future that science can promise! The brightest fantasy pales in comparison. But we are too busy even to consider it. We play with the dirt of earth and tend to forget everything else. Unfortunately, there exists a force that likes to exploit our carelessness, and this is Satan. He is the cause of our original trouble. He has authority over us, since Adam and Eve handed it to him. And he is wise. At one time he was the highest-ranking angel in the universe. He had a position just one step below God. He is powerful and resourceful in his lying. He even succeeded in seducing many angels when he attempted to overthrow God. He is the one who plants false ideas in our heads. He was the one who set science on a destructive course. He is the one who helped to invent the weapons that can eliminate half of mankind in mere hours. He is the cause of all our troubles, but his lies are transparent to those who search earnestly for truth. Since the sacrifice on Calvary, he hasn't had absolute power over us, unless we consent with our free will.

If we consider the possibility of this new, dimensional approach to the higher reality of the universe, then we will see how naive is any attempt to understand the full universe and God using the limited knowledge acquired by science so far. Science has some partial truths about our immediate surroundings, but when we leave that solid ground our knowledge is nothing but guesswork. We do not have the means to prove it either way. Any effort to find God using scientific methods is like the primitive statement of Khrushchev, who stated publicly that we have sent our astronauts to heaven and they found neither God nor the angels. All atheistic statements about the existence of God are only a variation on this infinitely stupid statement. They are like the ostrich who puts his head in the sand and believes that since he can't see the approaching enemy, the enemy can't see him either. We can't see God or the angels because our crude senses are not created to. Our sensors are unable to detect the reality of higher dimensions unless beings on those dimensions want to show themselves to us. Our heads are buried in the sand of matter, but this doesn't mean that higher reality does not exist. Those who deny the supernatural are only repeating the mistake of the ostrich.

In St. Thomas's imagination, which is the summation of all previous knowledge, the place for the fallen angels and their leader Satan, or Lucifer, was below the earth's crust. We don't really know just what this means. Since earth stands for little in the universe anymore, this may no longer be a sufficient explanation for hell. Jesus in some of His parables mentioned the outer darkness as the place of torment. The Bible many times refers to Satan as the Prince of Darkness, and apparently Satan himself likes this title, since it is frequently used in satanic cults. This might give us some ground for placing him in this expanded universe. We know that between the galaxies there are vast spaces, and that these spaces are not entirely empty. Some stars escaping from the galaxies find refuge there. Could this be the place of hell, this intergalactic space with its darkness and emptiness? It is possible, but who can be sure? From this place the dark forces could easily reach any part of the galaxy. There is a constant battle going on in the universe between God's forces and the forces of darkness; the center of this struggle is somehow our tiny planet earth. Human souls have a special function in this fight—we don't know exactly what it is, but both sides seek more and more human souls.

In this fight, there are many human casualties. Satan, since the victory over him in Calvary, no longer has absolute power over us, but he is still a formidable enemy, and without God's special protection nobody can resist his clever temptations. Jesus assured us that we needn't worry about our lives, that he can't take them, but He taught us that we should worry about our souls, and be afraid of those who are able to kill our souls. In our lives we seldom have to worry about threats to our physical life, but we should worry about our souls. The soul killers are everywhere, and their method is to promise pleasure to those who let them into their lives. A wholesale slaughter of souls is going on everywhere. Satan is using every conceivable tactic and method to harvest souls. One of his sharpest tools is science. Souls are killed before they are able to mature, to choose for themselves. Some call that education. God's laws are prohibited in the schools, but atheist dogmas are proclaimed as unquestionable truths.

Seeing the many criminal acts around us, one might say they

deserve a punishment. But we should think about our children—do we also wish them to suffer punishment for their sins? We all are God's children. Each soul is so dear to Him that He even took our punishment on Himself at Calvary to save us from eternal damnation. We don't have the faintest idea of what eternal damnation really means, but He knows, and He would like to save everybody from it. But even for God the rules are the rules, and our free will must prevail in the choice. He can't save us against our will. And He can't show Himself unless we want to find Him.

Compared with the new, dimensional image of the universe, all atheist imaginations based on our limited knowledge are primitive, at best. What can science offer against such a picture? We saw how uncertain our knowledge is, even in the most exact science, physics. We have reached our limit in the direction of the microcosmos, and we have to admit that we know virtually nothing about the macrocosmos, the realm of stars. Is this visual universe the basis of all dimensions? Possibly so, but even this universe is above our level of existence, for it is mostly composed of eternal energy, which must represent the fifth dimension. Matter is only a special manifestation of this energy, regardless of whether it is in the stars or in our body. Our body is composed of atoms, but we haven't the faintest idea just why and how these atoms, which are exactly identical to those in our surroundings, came together in such an unusual manner to separate us from the ground. We have discovered something about the large units of our body, about how they function, but that is almost nothing. It concerns only our animal part. Psychology, although its name boasts of dealing with our soul, actually manages to manipulate some of our animal instincts in a direction contrary to our interest, thus robbing us of our freedom of choice.

We saw how shaky our knoweldge of the past is. Actually, we aren't able to go further back in time than five or six thousand years. Even then we walk on thin ice. This time is apparently after the Great Flood, which swept away humankind as it existed previously and reshaped the surface of the earth, destroying all evidence of earlier times. Despite the fact that this event was recorded, atheists deny it, because it doesn't fit their theories. While they deny such proven facts, they place chance on their altars and worship it as their god. There is no such thing as chance. To say that events came into existence or happened by chance means that a process obeys laws unknown to us. Anyone who employs chance as a cause is openly confessing his ignorance.

If our knowledge of the past is so shaky, what about the future? What sort of future does this new religion promise us? In that regard, we can choose between Huxley's *Brave New World* and Harry Harrison's *Make Room, Make Room*, which was made into a film under the title *Soylent Green*. The modern theologians of this new religion are the science fiction writers, who dream about space colonies, starships roaming the universe at the speed of light. They forget that we aren't designed to do anything like that. The world of *Soylent Green* is our horrifying future; it is reality. Doctors are working feverishly to bring us eternal life, as alchemists worked centuries ago to produce the philosopher's stone that would enable its owner to change anything into gold. Alchemists failed, as genetic research is doomed to fail. Our lifespan is programmed into our genes, and no one will be able to change it, not even after a thousand years' research. We don't need to make our present form eternal. We, all of us, have eternal life; even those who don't admit it do. To get there, we have to undergo a change for the better, but the way to this is not through genetic research. It is a lot simpler—you need only believe. How foolish would a pupa be to resist the change to a butterfly, or an embryo, to prevent birth! Such an effort would mean the death of the embryo. It is the same with our unborn soul. Every such effort is bound to kill the soul.

Atheists fool themselves when they believe that with death everything ends abruptly. They, too, have an eternal soul, regardless of their beliefs. The awakening will be a frightening one. Their chosen master is the most cruel being in the universe. He is embittered by his constant failures and for his own consolation finds great pleasure in torturing the unfortunates who were foolish enough to believe in his lies. The most torturing thought, however, for the unfortunates will be the knowledge that they deceived themselves and lost a unique place in the universe that surpasses in joy and happiness the greatest imagination.

Eternity is more real than our brief life on earth. Recently, even scientific evidence of this has surfaced. Stories collected by doctors prove that we don't die with death, but only escape from an undesirable prison called our body and enter into a higher dimension. Those who have had a glimpse of this higher reality cannot find words to describe it. But this new reality won't be pleasant for everybody, although some books have misleading ideas about that. Patients who have experienced hell quite understandably are reluctant to talk about their experiences. How sad will be the awakening for those who bury their heads in the quicksand of materialism and atheism, believing in the false assurances of science! But those who successfully pass the hard test of life, which is eventually easy and tailored for each individual so as not to exceed his ability, will be rewarded with the crown of eternal life and the sonship of God, the highest possible place in the universe. For them there will no longer be limitations. They can realize the dream of the science fiction writers; they can travel all over the universe to see all its secrets; they can enjoy the company of God, the source of all knowledge; and they still won't be bored, because the universe is full of breathtaking surprises that will last forever. There is no way that our limited mind can comprehend anything of life in higher dimensions. Compared to it the most joyful moment of our lives is misery.

Science fiction writers project a future in which science elevates us to godhood, gives us eternal life. The reality is quite the opposite of this. We all die together, along with these new prophets. I must admit that they are sometimes very entertaining, but despite this innocent mantle these modern fairy tales are very dangerous. They are nothing but an effective vehicle for atheistic ideas. The continuous repetition of these tales has a brainwashing effect, especially on youth. Most of them have never heard of God, or if they did they find religion boring compared to these fairy tales. This is exactly the effect that the atheists want to achieve. So far, a couple of generations have grown up who believe in the tales of science fiction and know nothing about God.

How can we perceive God? We must admit it is impossible. He is so far above us that the greatest flight of fantasy falls back with broken wings. In spite of this, God reveals Himself to those who patiently and humbly search for Him. Though God is one, the perceived image of Him differs in time and with the individual. Despite these differences, all the images are true, because only a minute fraction of God is imaginable. Many factors can influence our perception of God. God is everywhere yet nowhere. The vast amount of energy constituting the universe is only a part of Him. The atoms, which we learned are only energy confined to tiny spaces, are also part of Him, but they aren't God either. We are part of Him, too. Our souls represent a spark of God, but we still aren't God. We are His sons, but only after our death can we receive our inheritance, depending on how we took the test of life. He wants all of us, but many of us don't want Him, and He respects our choice. Many of us forget that we are only on a journey home. How many of us never reach the gates!

Though it is distressing to see those unfortunates who fall victim to Satan, and as his obedient servants try to ruin our lives, too, we should rather pity them, as Jesus did even on the cross, because they know not what they do. If they could comprehend reality as it is, they would be on their knees day and night to avert the terrible fate awaiting them after death. The reality of hell can't be explained away with scientific arguments. Today they laugh at us, but for how long? Imagine what sort of fate will await those teachers who deliberately lead astray countless young souls. In our time, when Christianity is gradually fading away and being forced out of our lives, the ancient question, Was Jesus the Son of God? has resurfaced. It is being debated, not only by the secular world, but even by theologians. The new worldview based on science favors those who conceive of Jesus as only a good man. Such opinions are preached in many churches, leading many astray. Most educated men embrace this false theory. They admit that there must be some great force behind the universe, which we call God, but incarnation? It doesn't make sense. It is for the superstitious only.

But what if they are wrong? Jesus said: "I am the way

and the truth, and the life; no one comes to the Father, but by me." If this is true—and we firmly believe it is—then what will be the fate of those skeptics? Their fate will be worse than that of openly militant atheists, because they know what they do—they are serving their master, while atheists really know not what they do. Many of them are good men, leading exemplary lives, fit even to be good Christians, and yet they still will be lost because they were too lazy to find the way and the truth, and thus they will never arrive home. Many of them put their faith in others' opinions, and don't even bother to look for the truth themselves. They are the most pitiable among mankind. They are sheep led by blind pastors to the slaughter.

We believe that Jesus is the incarnate second person of the Godhead. One of his tasks was to bring us closer to God, whose name was previously unpronounceable. He taught us to call God with confidence "Our Father." By lowering himself to our humanity, He lifted us up to such a height that for us heaven is reachable. How much more could one ask? Neither technology nor knowledge will elevate us to godhood, but faith alone. This faith must be so great that we completely abandon ourselves, like the drowning man to his rescuer in order to be saved by Him. God always does the very best for those who leave the choice to Him. But in science and technology, we have set out to reach salvation without Him.

Jesus brought God close to us. In the early period of Christianity, this new image of God was translated into pictures and statues by artists to aid those who had less vivid imaginations. God sometimes was projected as an old human father figure with white hair and beard, but this later became a stumbling block for many. Protestantism went to the other extreme. They threw out every statue and picture from their churches. Nietzsche, the mad atheist philosopher, describes how the image of God changed for him from a lovely godfather figure to a cruel and powerless being.

The truth is that we can't perceive God. The public image of God is also subject to change. As we saw, our imagination of God must change if we consider the expanded knowledge of our universe. But this doesn't mean that God Himself changes. He is unchangeable throughout the ages and even eternity. What changes is our perception of Him. In this expanded universe we have to correct our perception of God if we don't want to deceive ourselves. But seeing this vastly expanded universe, which is only His creation, this increased knowledge must make us humble. Most real scientists become very humble as their knowledge increases. Science has nothing against God. It is only used astutely and falsely against Him by exploiting the failures of our images of Him in previous ages. But this by no means can be used as proof against the existence of God or against His undeniable truths revealed through the prophets in the Bible. As we saw, the Bible can even enhance our limited scientific knowledge. Besides, the vast universe is so perfect, even in minute details, that we must admire the Maker of all these wonders. No, chance has nothing to do with our universe. It is more perfect than that; besides, no such thing as chance exists! Wouldn't it be better for those lazy souls to look for the truth while they can, and not let themselves be deceived by others?

CONCLUSION

In this book, we examined the most important branches of science in search of evidence to support the atheists' claim that science proves that the idea of God and religion belongs to the realms of myths and legends, and that it is based on the superstitious ignorance of men of previous ages. We found that no such proofs exist. Instead, we found that our knowledge is very limited, and is increasingly uncertain when we depart from the solid ground of our immediate surroundings.

In both directions, toward both the microcosmos and the macrocosmos, we have reached the limit of our ability to penetrate. We discovered that in both directions we can reach the realm of energy, which is unknowable for us. It may turn out that energy represents the fifth dimension.

It is widely held today that time represents the fourth dimension. If we can accept that, it tells us our most basic limitation in this human form, that we do not exist in this dimension. We can have some limited knowledge of the past by reconstructing events, but our reconstructions will never be accurate, and thus contradictory explanations are possible. As for just what the future holds, we have no idea other than that religious prophecies can offer.

Atheism is a negative view of life. It restricts and senselessly bounds even our limited ability to understand the universe. It represents a very low level of thinking. It is a product of limited minds that are unable to perceive things other than those a few primitive senses can detect. While religion tries to lift man to higher dimensions, pointing out phenomena that clearly indicate the existence of realities beyond our material world, atheism, in opposition to this effort, tries to drag man down to a level of existence below even the animals.

Both we and our dwelling place, earth, are unique phenomena in the universe. But we aren't alone. The universe is populated by beings somewhat similar to us but existing in higher dimensions. Religion—a summary of knowledge communicated to us by those beings—explains our situation clearly. According to it, our ancestors once also belonged to the higher dimensions, but they lost their status as a consequence of disobedience to the Creator. But we know also that after a short period of time, a pilgrimage on earth, we can regain our previous status or even a higher one, since we have the possibility of becoming the sons of God, a status even higher than that of the angels.

We know also that in a sense we were victims of a higher power opposing God. This is the reason God didn't sentence us more harshly and gave us the opportunity of regaining our previous status, while He was more severe with Satan and his followers. The mere fact that Satan, or Lucifer, was able to organize a rebellion against God shows us that he must be a very powerful being, on a dimension not much less than that of God Himself. Since we joined him, he has jurisdiction over us. Jesus Christ, however, purchased us the freedom of choice. Satan now has no power over us, unless through our free will we give it to him. Although the choice is ours, Satan uses every means of deception to divert us from reaching our goal. Satan's tactics change through the ages and according to each individual. Today his deadliest weapon is science, wherein he can successfully mix lies with truth. Only a few are able to penetrate deep enough into science to separate truth from lies. Science is purposefully blown out of proportion today. Specialization, with its avalanche of details, is able to bury the most brilliant minds, not to mention those who know science only from atheist propaganda.

Since science doesn't have any proof to support the atheists' claims, the use of science against God is a trick. With this lie Satan is able to divert many potential sons of God from reaching their destiny, and with their full consent reclaim them as his slaves for eternity. Most of the unfortunate persons blinded by satanic lies dressed in the robe of scientific truth neglect to look at the other side of the coin, to search for the truth themselves. They base their eternal fate on other men's opinions. They know nothing of God's truth, basically because they are too lazy to look for it. Today, when life is being taken over by the servants of Satan, and God is gradually being excluded, it has become increasingly difficult to search for truth. God has been expelled from the schools, and many people can't even find Him in the churches. Even if someone develops an interest, there are few books on the subject that are able to convince a skeptic, who may have inherited his skepticism or disbelief from his parents. Theologians are also caught in the web of Satan and his scientific lies, and many of them are unable to offer any solution to disperse skepticism. Some of them have even become victims and spread the darkness. "Higher Criticism" is only their skepticism dressed in a scientific mantle.

Recently, science began to be interested in the supernatural. But science approaches the question from a wrong direction when it identifies the supernatural with the occult, black magic, and witchcraft. Through these efforts Satan would like to emerge from the denial of even his own existence and establish himself over mankind as a god.

Atheists would like us to believe that life ends with death. But it doesn't, not even for them! We all have eternal life, and death means only a changing of form. But, according to the rule established by God, our fate after death in the new form will be determined by the outcome of the test that is the real meaning of our life on earth. This is the entrance examination, and whosoever fails to pass it will be banished. All of us are invited, but only a few are chosen. The higher beings don't leave us in ignorance of what fate awaits those who fail this test. One may argue that it isn't fair to punish those who failed, but no such argument can alter the reality. Everyone has all the necessary knowledge or tools to pass it successfully. Everyone has an equal opportunity, regardless of race, sex, or national origin. God is the most equal of equal-opportunity employers! The test is even tailored to individual ability. It is carefully monitored so that no one is tested beyond his ability. The test is completely fair, but it is only an opportunity. Christ lifted us up to such a height that everybody can reach heaven, but He can't give you the final push if you resist. If someone is not interested, it is his business; no one will be forced against his own free will.

Don't you think that a person ought to make every effort to make sure he chooses the right path in life? To know both sides before he decides, since the stakes are so high? Those who can believe instinctively in God or who learn religion from their parents are fortunate. Gaining faith by reason is harder, but it is not impossible. It requires, however, much hard work, and an open mind without prejudice. This book can be the start of such an effort. It also can be a guiding light for scientists to clean up their fields and free science from the bondage and slavery of atheism. The tide is turning; we are beyond the ignorant period of the last century's militant atheists. Science no longer supports them. Quite the contrary, it supplies us with ever-increasing evidence that they were wrong. Our world is more complex than we previously thought, and to understand it requires a Creator.

While I was writing this conclusion I received an unexpected confirmation of my ideas about the uncertainties of our knowledge. *U.S. News and World Report* in its January 26, 1981, issue, published a conversation with M. Kline, professor emeritus of mathematics at New York University. During the last one hundred years, science elevated mathematics almost to the status of fetish. Anything that could be expressed in mathematical form was regarded as proven beyond the shadow of a doubt. The professor lately published a book, *Mathematics: The Loss of Certainty*. The title itself confirms just how uncertain our knowledge is, even in those areas that previous ages considered most precise. In the interview, the professor mentioned that mathematics was considered the most precise science a hundred years ago, capable of describing the universe accurately. As we went deeper, however, this certainty vanished. Today there is no agreement, even in basic principles. There are four different schools, which hold different views of the fundamental principles of mathematics. The professor sees this disagreement as a natural development, and asks why we should hold fast to one theory. Theories are man-made, artificial explanations, not the truth. Thus they are subject to change. To hold a theory sacrosanct, as the atheists hold Darwinism, is an obstacle to further development, as I have tried to prove. Kline thus advocates encouraging different schools of thought, on grounds that the competition eventually becomes the motor of progress in science.

The world is a lot more complex than it was thought to be in the last century. Some people can accept the concept of a Creator, but are unable to accept the truth of religion, particularly Christianity. It is hard to understand why. If God was able to create the universe, why is He not able to care about it, and, within it, us? He was certainly able to communicate the truth to us—it is recorded in the Bible—and He should be able to communicate with us even more in these times. It's hard to imagine that even He had to pay the price for our freedom, but this is how it happened. The rules are the rules even for Him, thus He had to send his Son, not as God, but as a sacrificial lamb to expiate our sins, so that we could become His sons once again. Why couldn't one accept the fact that even God had to pay the price to purchase our freedom from Satan's slavery? Jesus promised us that the punishment would end in due time. After the punishment, man will regain his previous status and much more under the leadership of God Himself, who paid the price for us, who purchased us on Calvary from Satan's slavery. The history of all of humankind is so short in the geological scale that the whole punishment, which seems to us very long, is only a very mild sentence compared with eternity. Those who can accept this basic truth have only one further step to make: they must study religion to be able to obtain the detailed map of how one can secure a place for himself among the sons of God. Neither science nor technology can furnish us with this information. Neither of them will lift mankind to godhood.

Perhaps this book will provoke some wandering souls to undertake their own search for the truth. A pitched battle is being waged above us between the forces of darkness and the forces of light. In this struggle a soul is a trophy, a scalp. Do you wonder where your scalp will come to rest?

SELECTED BIBLIOGRAPHY

1. Albright, W. F. : *From the Stone Age to Christianity.* 1957
   Doubleday Anchor Books

2. Filed, A. N. : *The Evolution Hoax Exposed.* 1971
   TAN BOOKS AND PUBLISHERS, INC.
   P.O. Box 424, Rockford, Ill. 61105

3. Harrison, H. : *Make Room, Make Room*, 1967
   Berkeley Medalion Books.

4. Heyerdahl, T. : *Kon-Tiki.* 1950
   Rand McNally & Co.

5. Huxley, A. : *Brave New World*, 1969
   Harper & Row

6. Huxley, A. : *Brave New World Revisited*, 1965
   Harper & Row

7. Mindzsenty, J. : *Memoires*, 1974
   Macmillan Publishing Co.

8. Velikovsky, I. : *Worlds in Collision*, 1972
   Dell Publishing Co.

9. Velikovsky, I. : *Earth in Upheaval*, 1968
   Dell Publishing Co.

10. White, A. D. : *A History of the Warfare of Science with Theology in Christendom*, 1965
    Macmillan Co.

DEAR FRIEND IN CHRIST:

If God allowed you to see the truth in this book, you may know someone else who can benefit from reading it.

Won't you recommend it to your friends and relatives and perhaps to the bookstore nearby?

In this way you can give me / an unworthy tool of God / a helping hand in reaching out for more souls, who perhaps can be saved.

Your effort may be rewarded by the one who is the only way and the truth.

The author

Books can be ordered from:
ATLAS BOOKS PUBLISHING COMPANY
P.O. Box 844
Mountain View, CA 94042

QUANTITY DISCOUNT PRICES:

1 copy	$4.98
2 copies	$4.00 each
3-5 copies	$3.50 each
5-25 copies	$3.00 each
25-50 copies	$2.75 each
60 and over	$2.50 each

For single copies kindly add $1 for postage and handling.

ORDER FORM:

Gentlemen:

Please send me _____ copies of THE APPLE OF KNOWLEDGE by Stephen A. Foglein.

Enclosed is my payment in the amount of _____
/ Check or money order /

Name _____

Street _____ City _____

State_____ Zip Code _____

ABOUT THE AUTHOR

Stephen A. Foglein was born in Hungary in 1936. The effort of atheistic, communist schools to infuse students with scorn for religion produced in him exactly the opposite, a deep faith in God. From his early youth he conscientiously strove to solve the contradiction between atheistic science and religion.

In the turbulent year of 1956, with God's special help, he was admitted to the Technical University of Heavy Industry in Miskolc, as a student of the Faculty of Mining Engineering, after a years work in a coal mine. The university is one of the oldest technical institutes in Central Europe, established in 1735. He finished his studies in 1961 and was awarded the MS degree in Mining and Geological Engineering. He has worked as an engineer in Hungary and in the United States, and is now an American citizen.

Besides his work as an engineer, Foglein has conducted intensive private research on the subject of historical geology, into theories of the origin of the earth and the solar system, and in astronomy, especially cosmology. He has never ceased his search for a key to unlock the artificial and unncessary controversy between today's science and religion.

This book, Foglein's second, is the result of that search. It can shed new light on all of our knowledge.

ALSO BY THIS AUTHOR

THE AGE OF "ONE FOLD AND ONE SHEPHERD" IS COMING:

An Analysis of World Events Based on Biblical and Christian Prophecies

Stephen A. Foglein

Like a cautious navigator on a turbulent sea, the author determines our place in history, on the seas of time.

There is much controversy and confusion in our time. Many proclaim the end of the world and the second coming of Jesus Christ, thus raising unfounded expectations. The author, after a long and careful search, concludes that this is not the case. God repeatedly warned us about this turbulent time we live in: Bible prophecies are being fulfilled before our very eyes; we hear about "wars and rumors of wars." But as Jesus said, "See that ye be not troubled. For these things must come to pass, but the end is not yet."/Matt.24:6/. Never in history could a war have been connected with the possible end of the world. Thus we can safely conclude that Jesus's warning was intended for us. This is what the messangers of God tell us throughout the ages. Our time is saturated with satanic influence to the point of no return. If God does not interfere, Satan and his followers will soon succeed in chasing God out of our life.

The fast approaching nuclear war will not extinguish life on Earth, as many prophets of the world proclaim. Our prophets assure us that the most happy era is in store for a great many of the survivors. All nations become Christian, and there will be only "one fold and one shepherd." These Christian prophecies, neglected by many, clarify and update the meaning of the Biblical prophecies, in complete harmony with them.

This happy era will end with the arrival of Antichrist and the last seven years of history, when the people of earth again turn against God. This will be the time of the second coming of Jesus Christ, the consumation of the world and the General Judgment.

The book is a fascinating and objective analysis of what is going on around us and why from God's point of view, a needed and very readable guide for everyone not afraid of the truth. It gives the reader a total understanding of world events from an historical perspective. A book you long have been waiting for.

The book is priced to reach as many souls as it can, at $4.95/paper, 189 pages.

Order your copy from:
Atlas Books Publishing Company
P.O. Box 844, Mountain View, CA 94042
Please kindly add one dollar for postage and handling.
Or ask for the book at your bookstore.

7 Days — God made earth.
6 days = 6,000 years almost since. M Hug Millenieder!
7 deep = 1 day is like 1,000!
These 6 days so few. and what can be found of Bones
Dugs in ground = do 6,000 years? prove?